SWEET D~~

COLORING BOOK
Grayscale

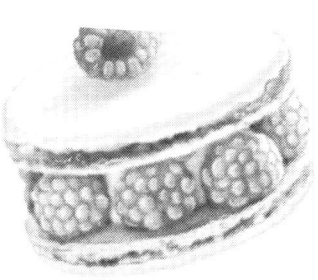

includes TWO full sets
of the 23 amazing illustrations

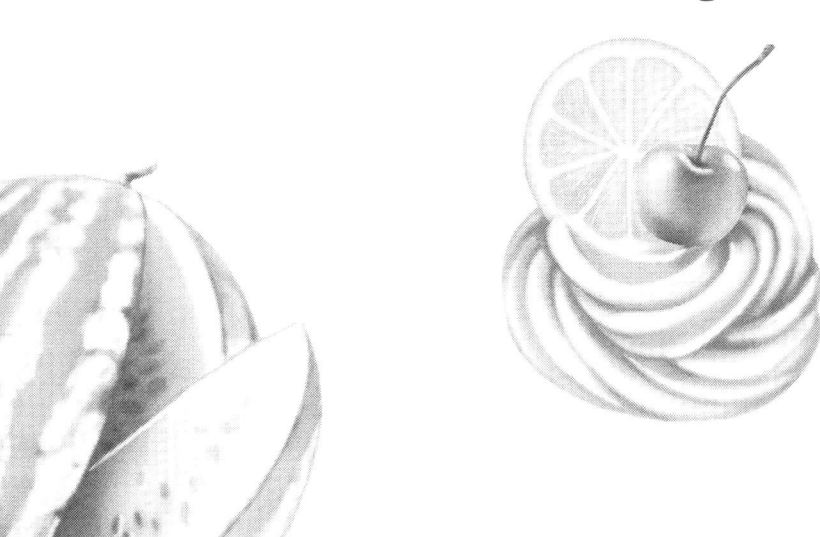

BONUS
7 pictures from
Alena Lazareva's other coloring books

Artworks by

Alena Lazareva

www.alenalazareva.com

Happy coloring!

Share Your Work

Alena Lazareva's Colouring Club

A group for sharing images, inspiration, tips, techniques
and more for Alena Lazareva colouring books:
www.facebook.com/groups/alenalazareva/

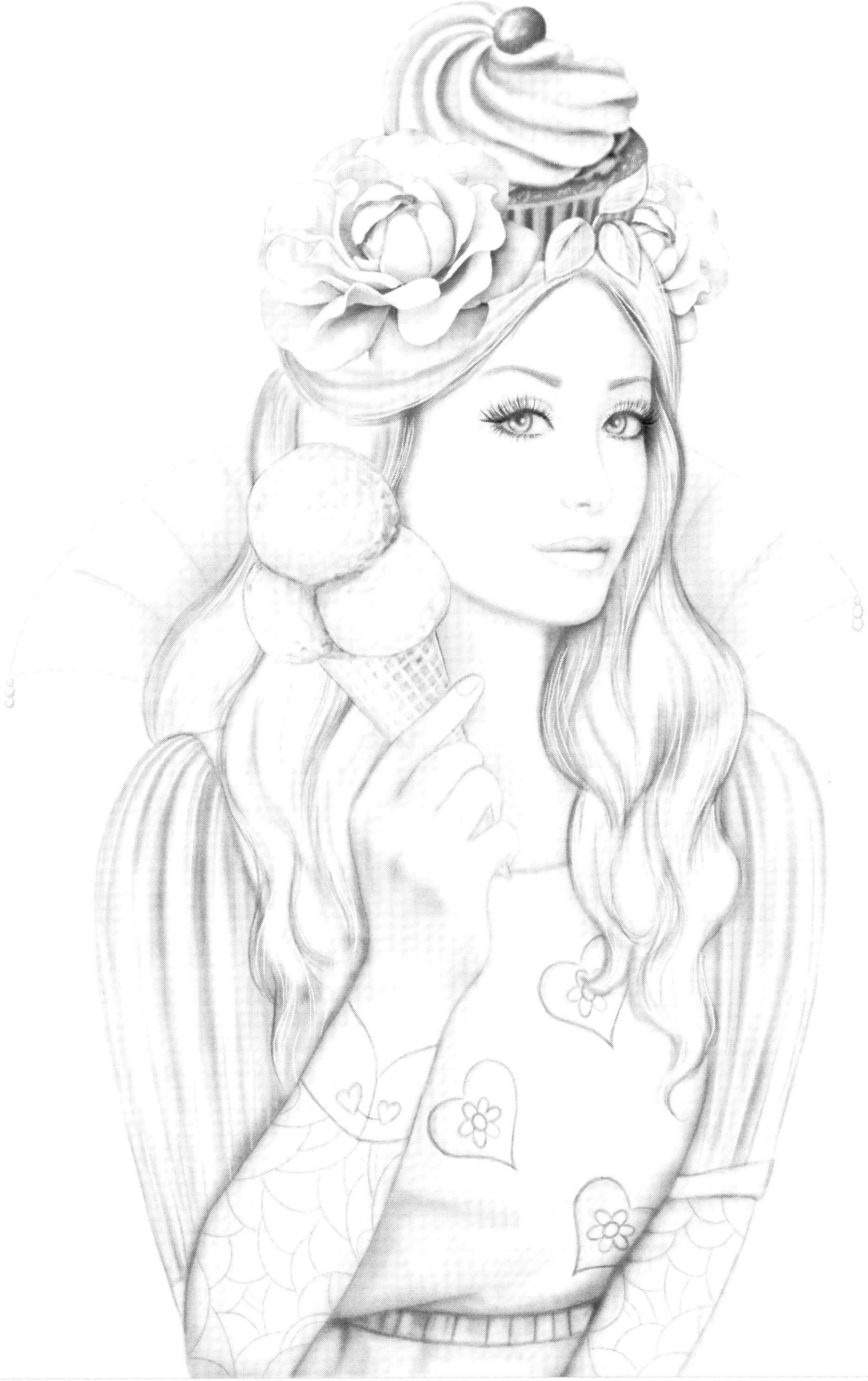

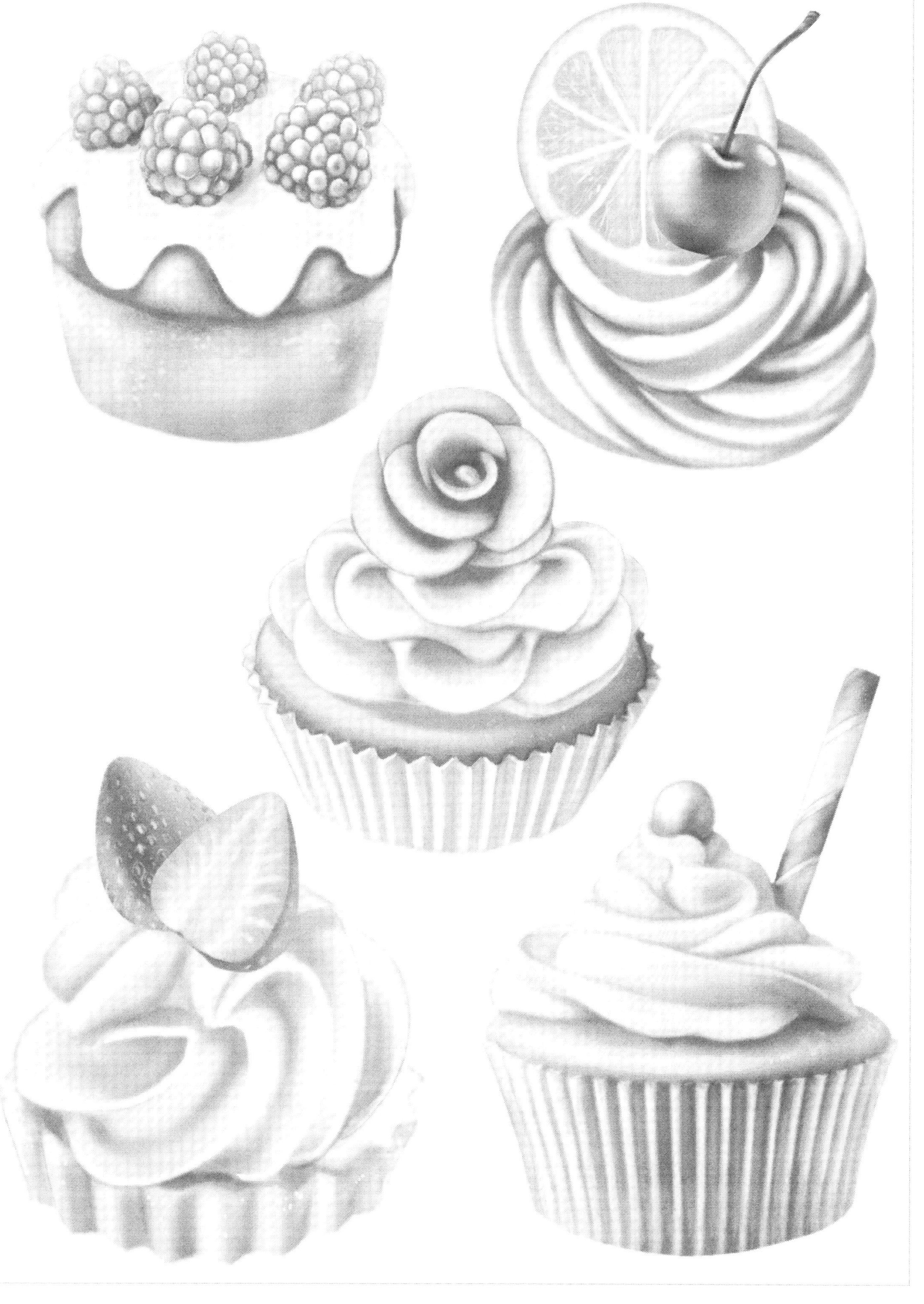

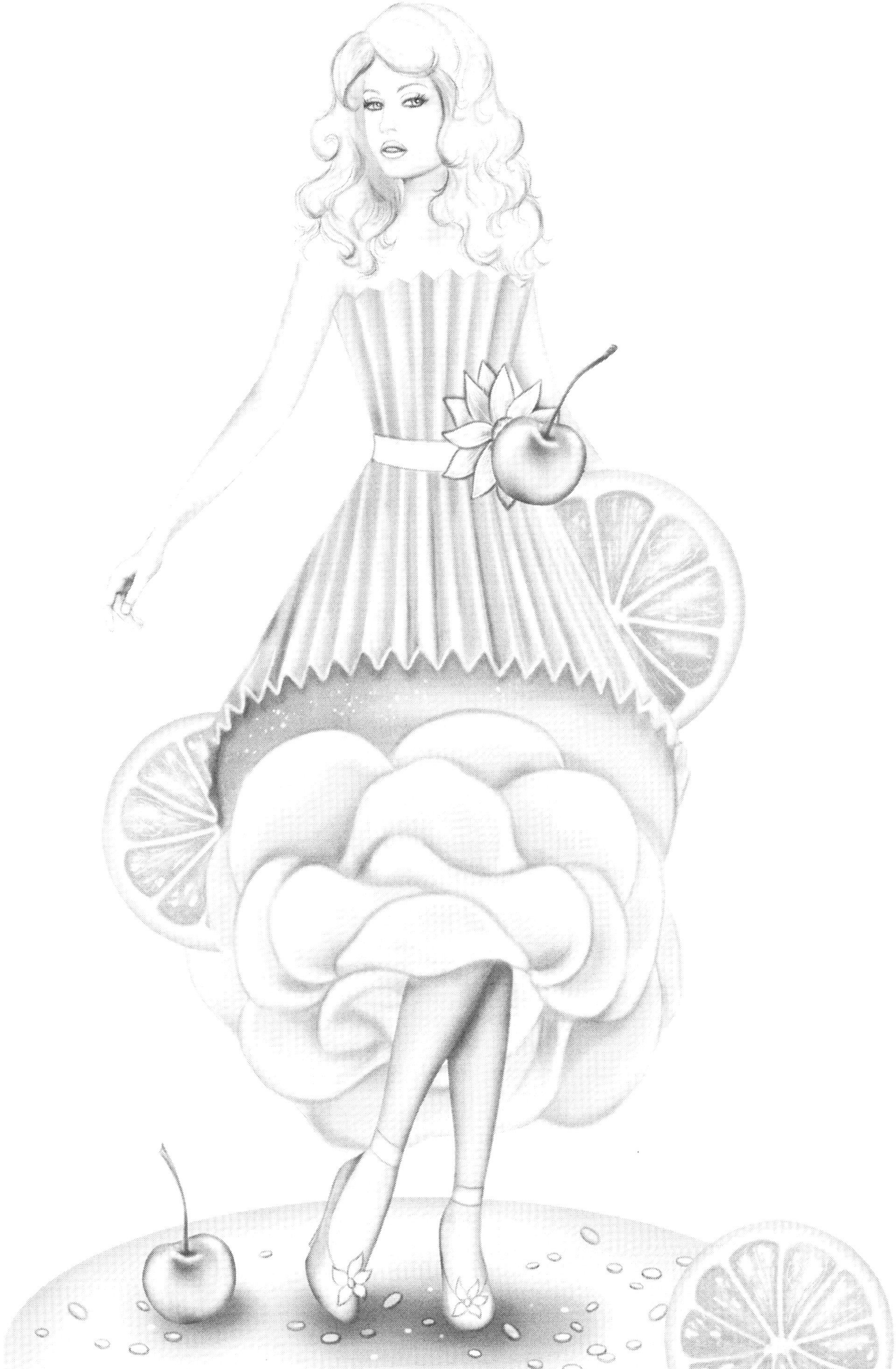

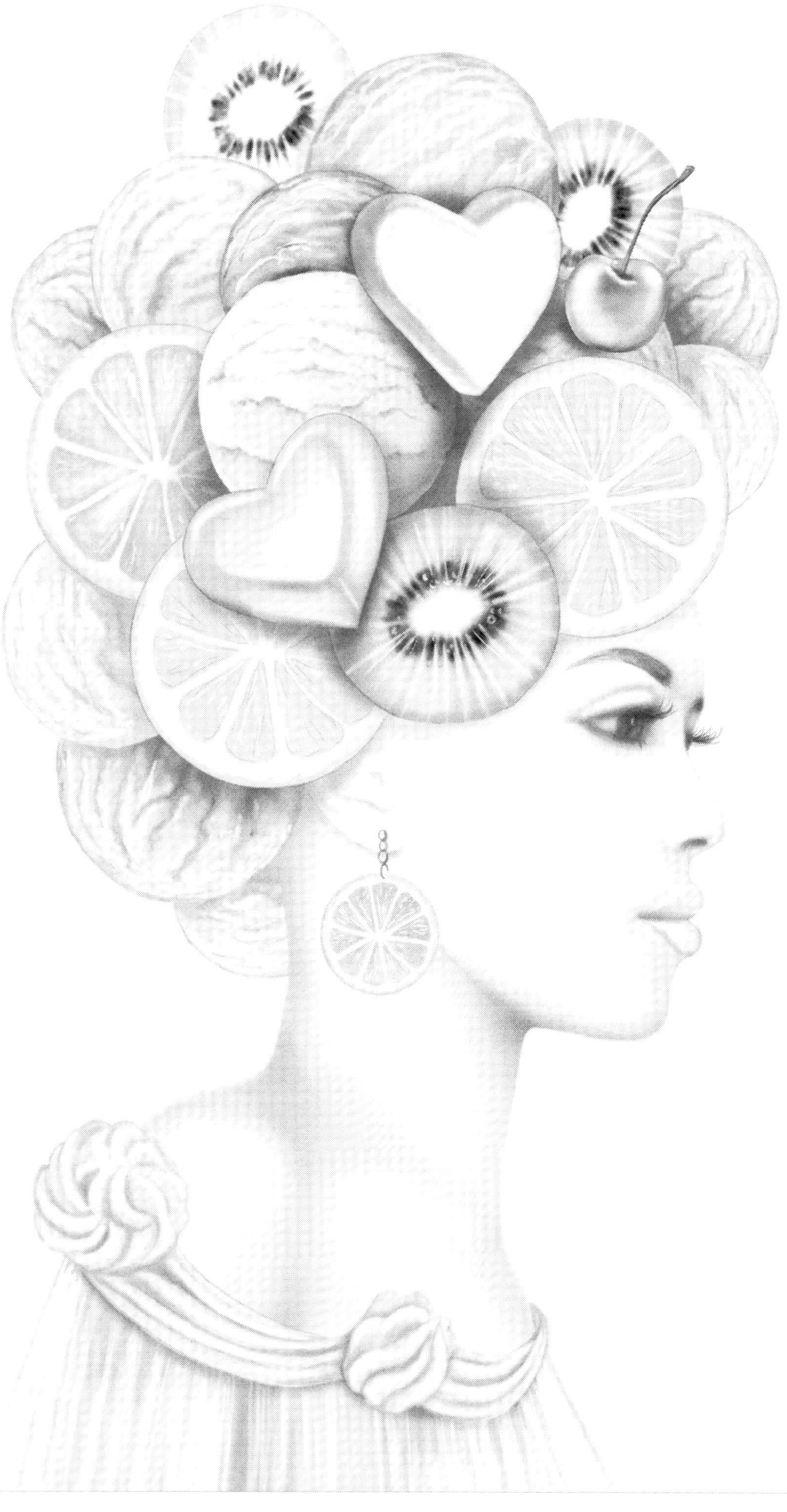

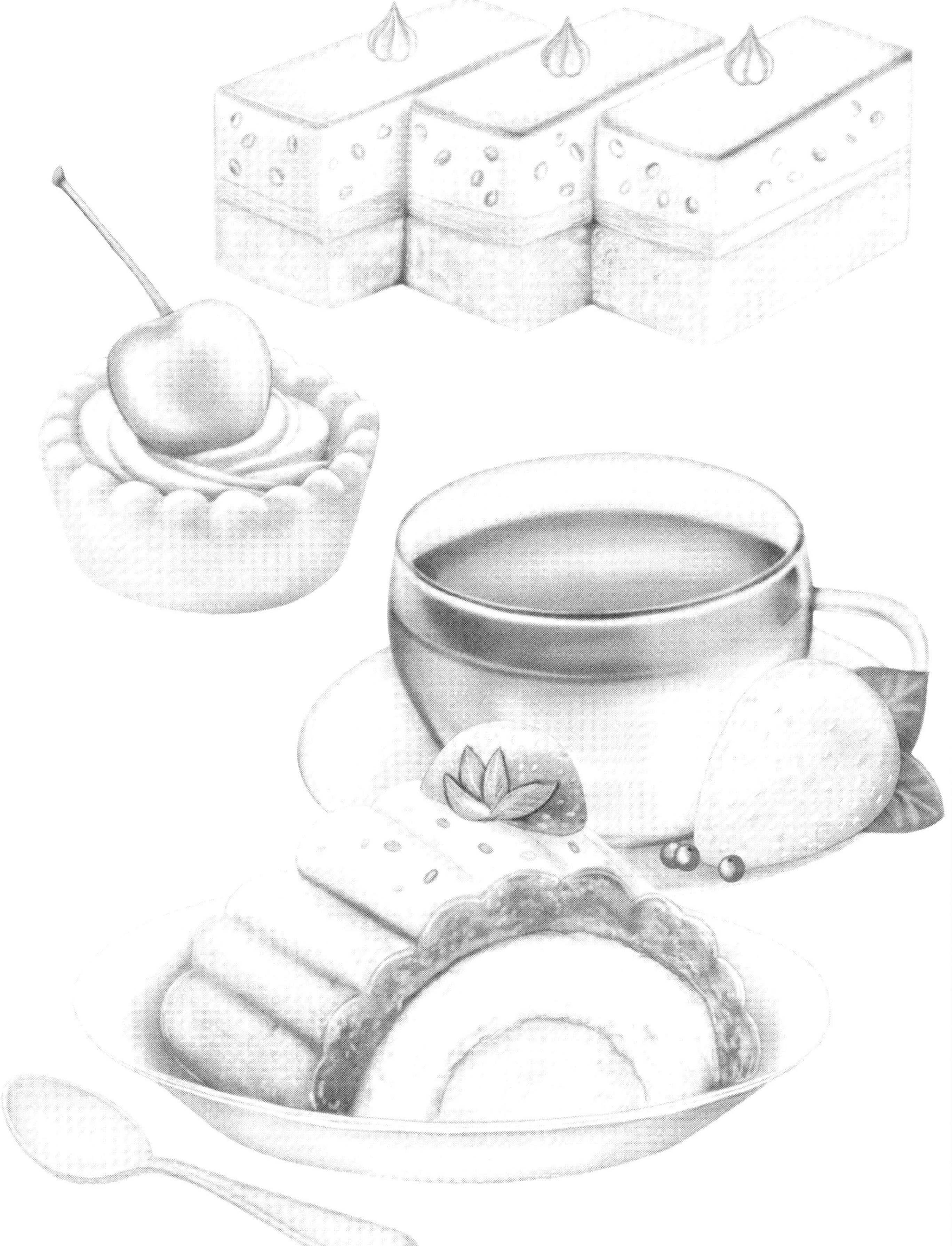

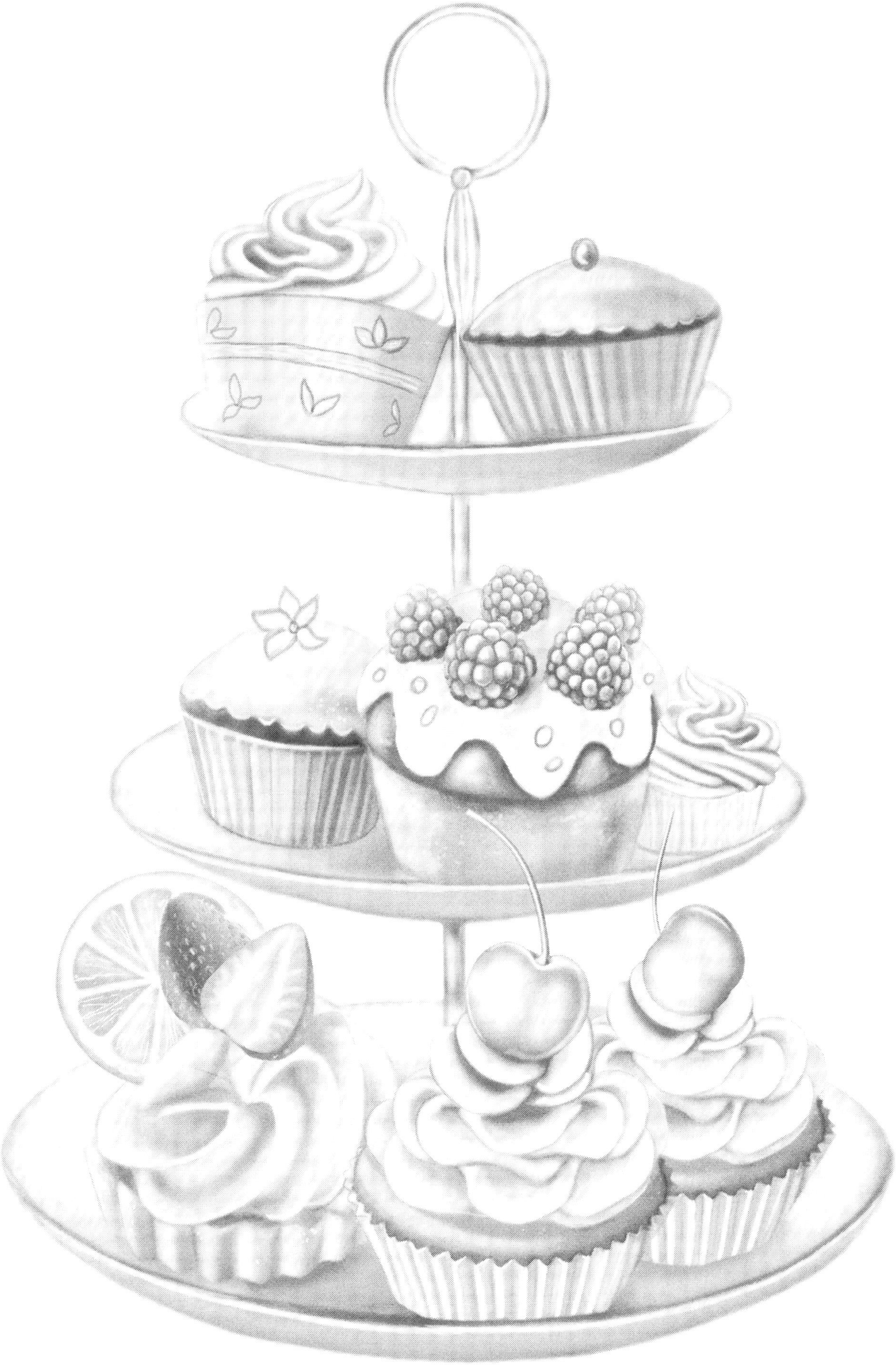

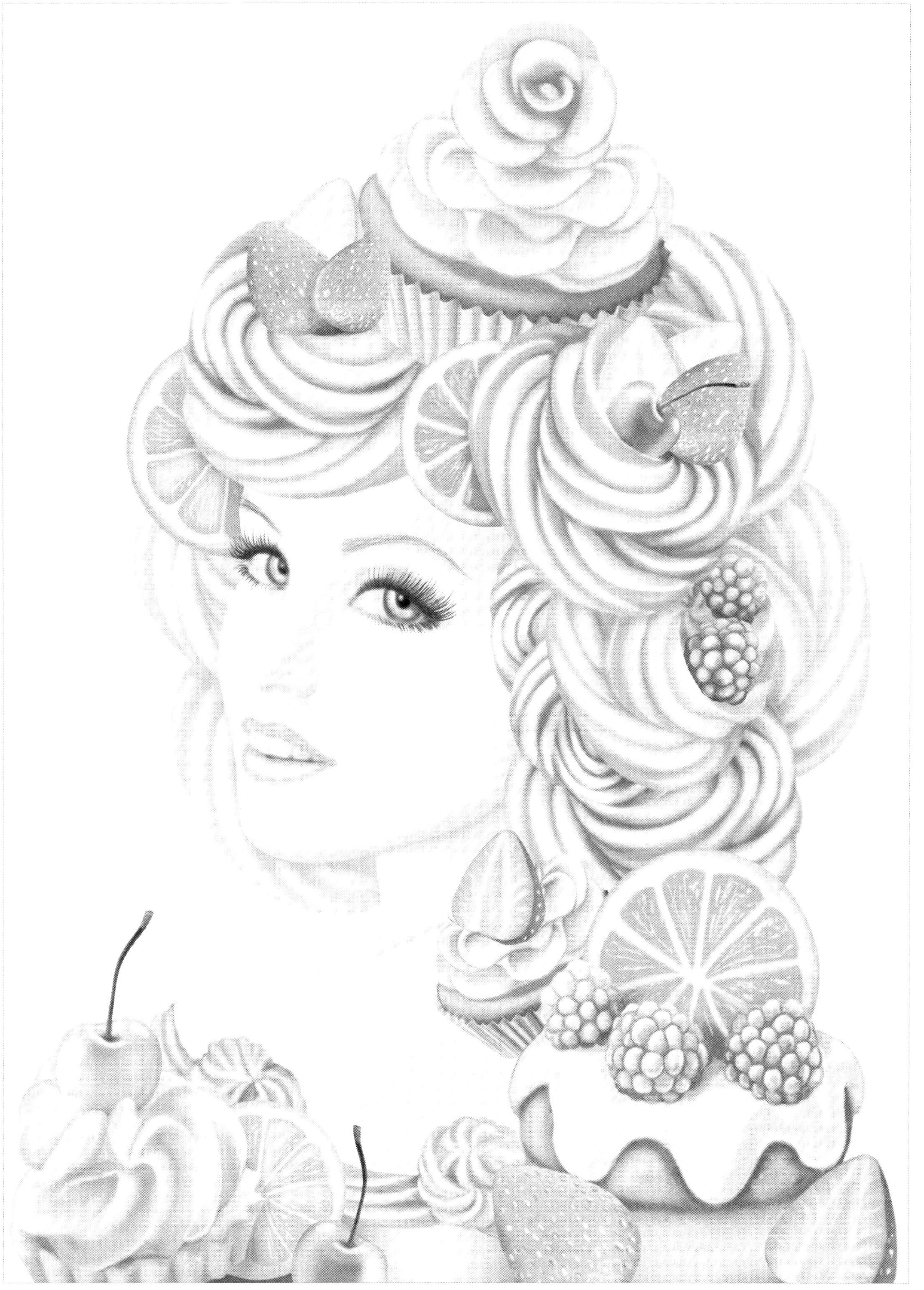

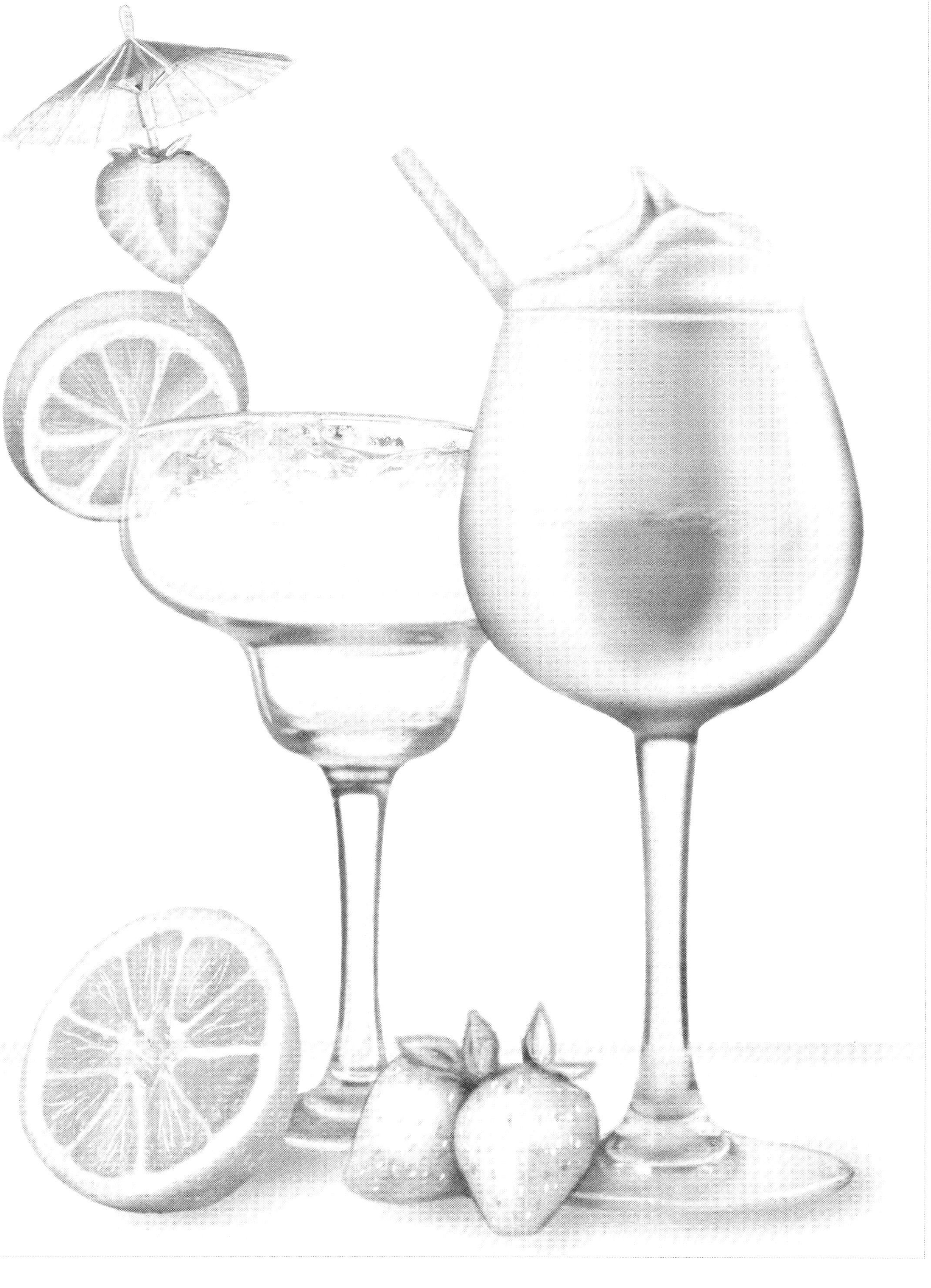

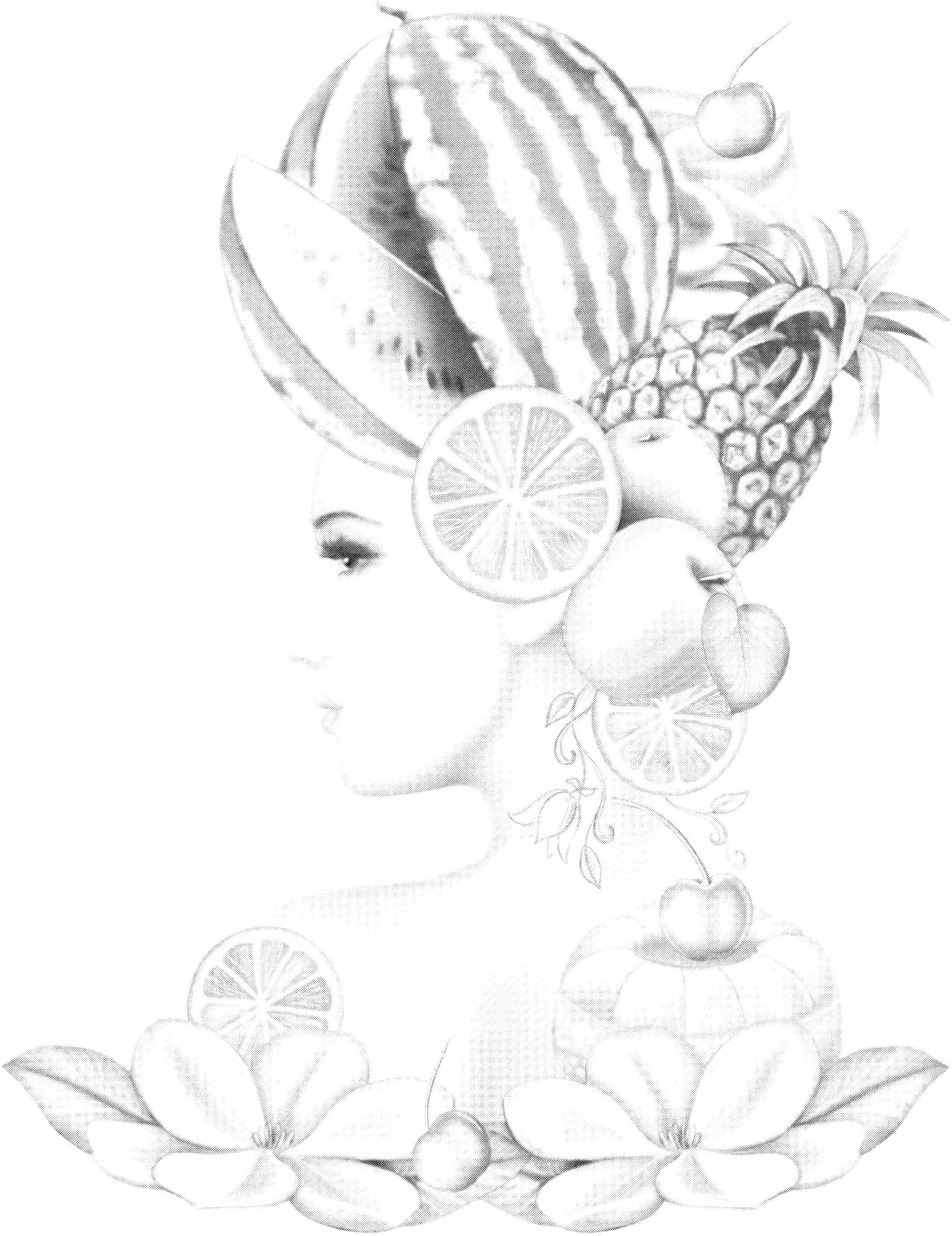

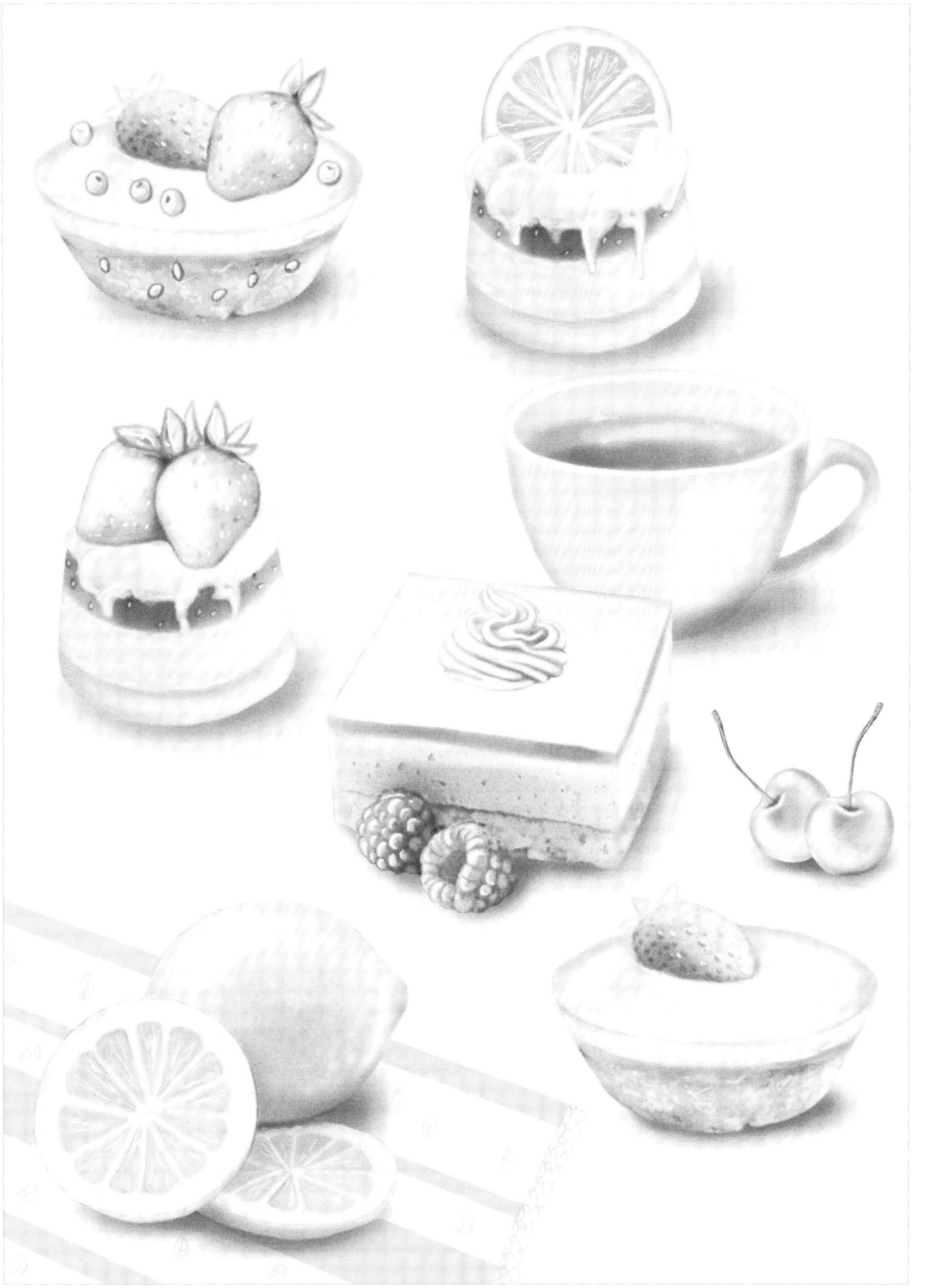

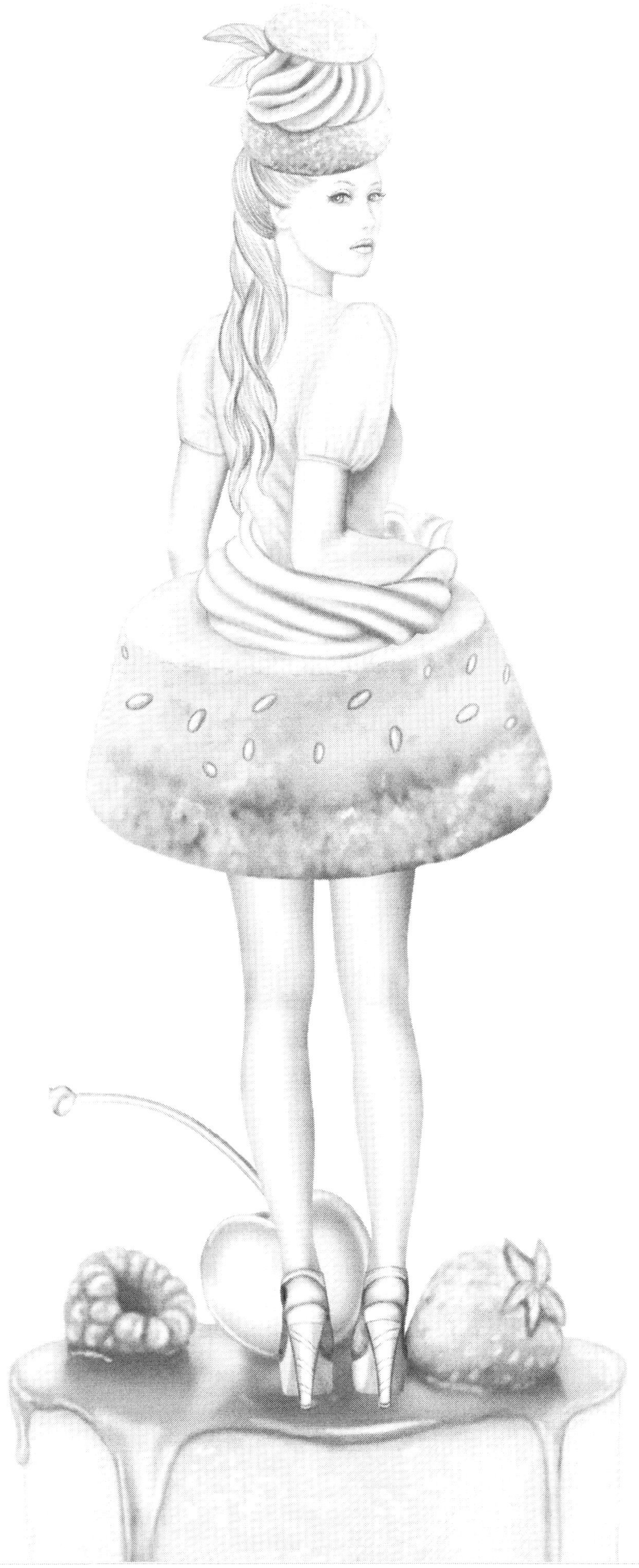

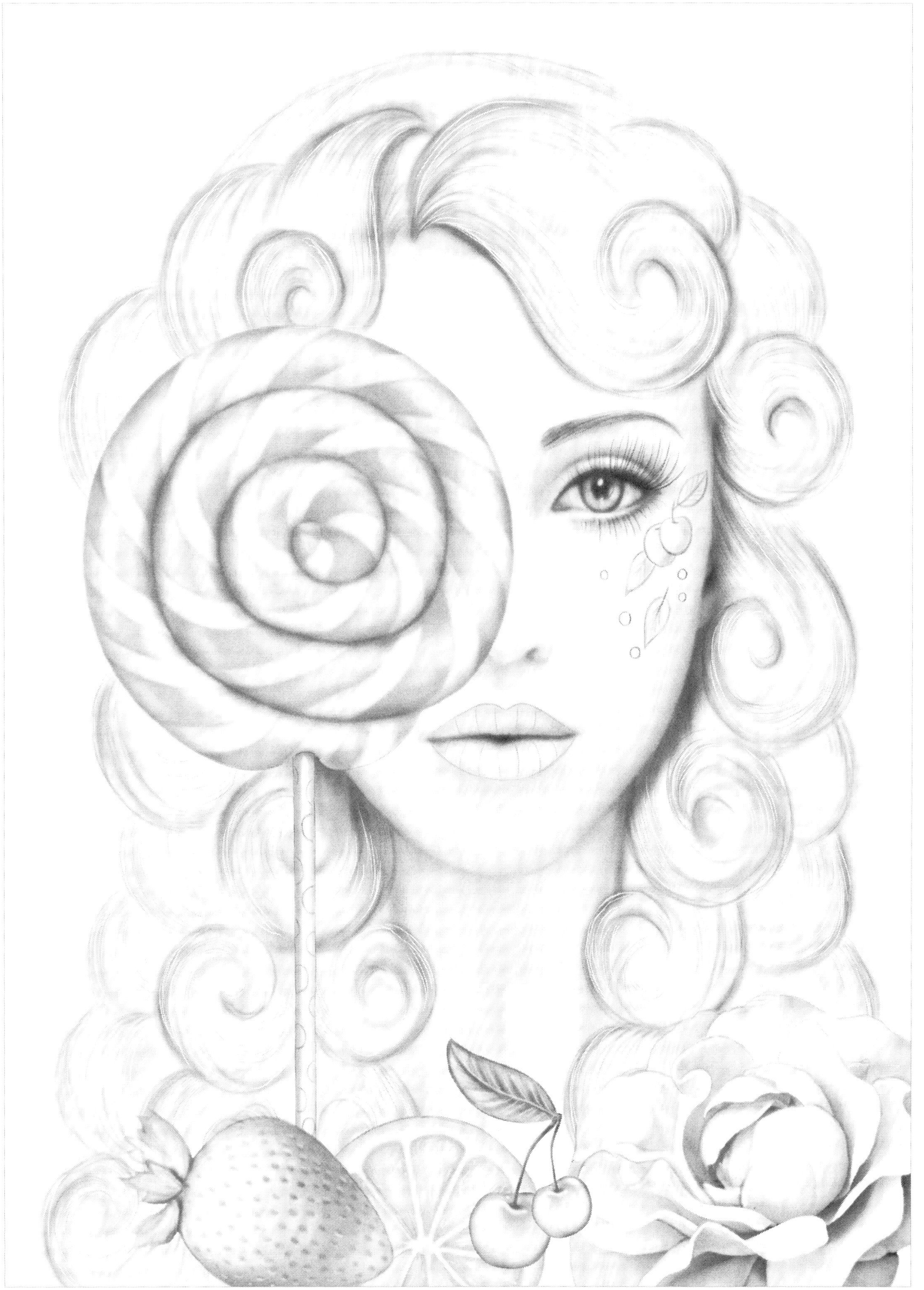

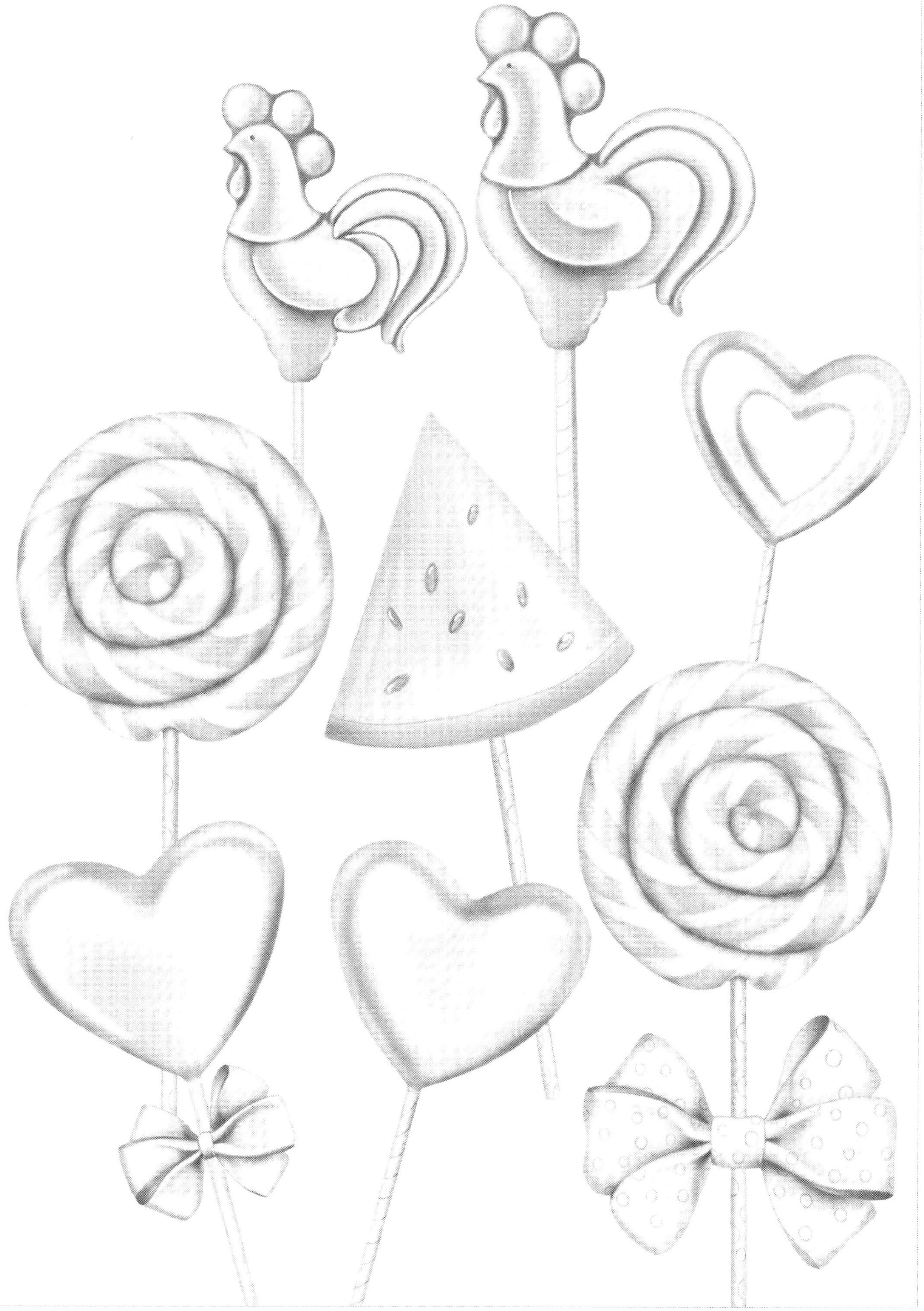

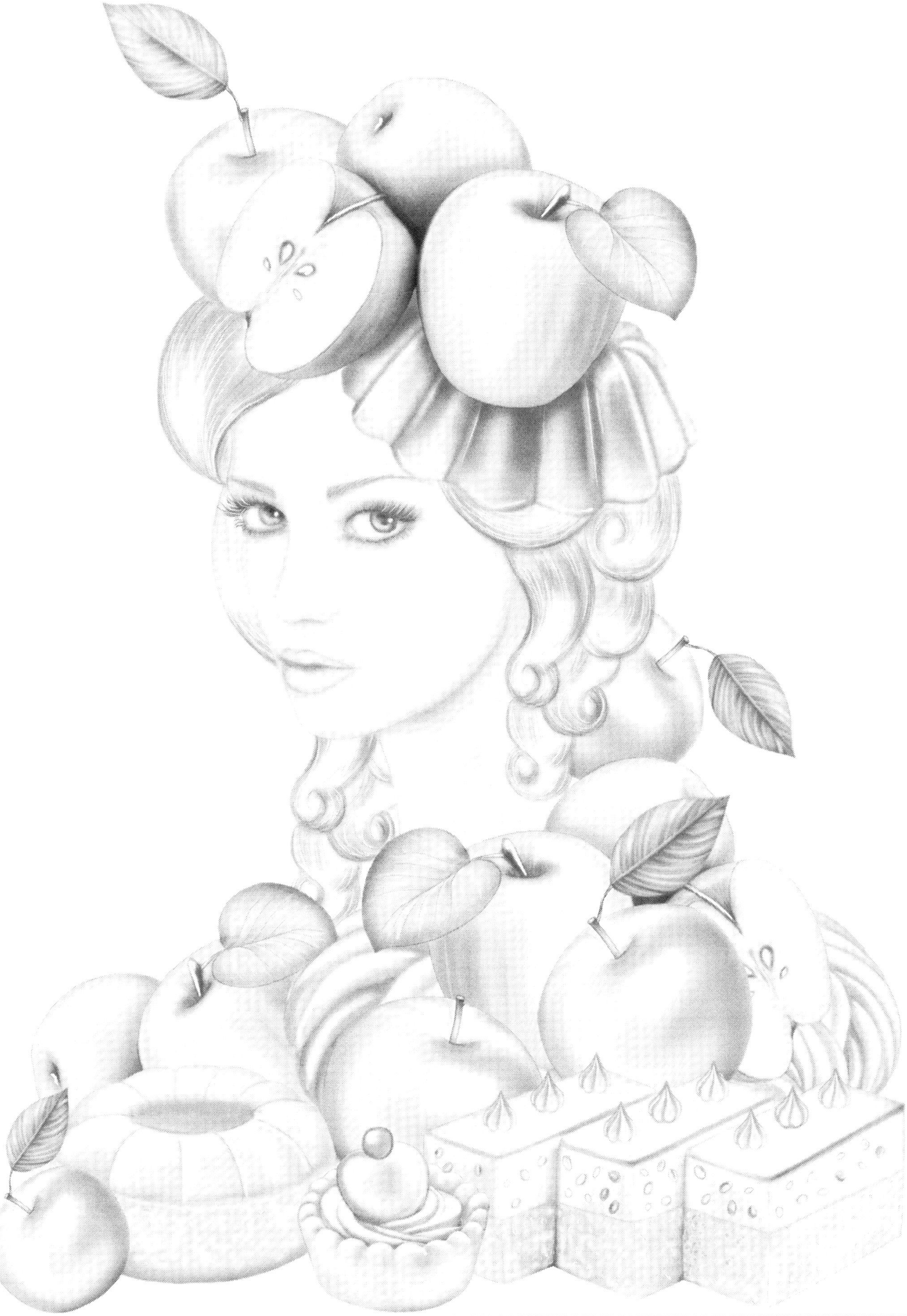

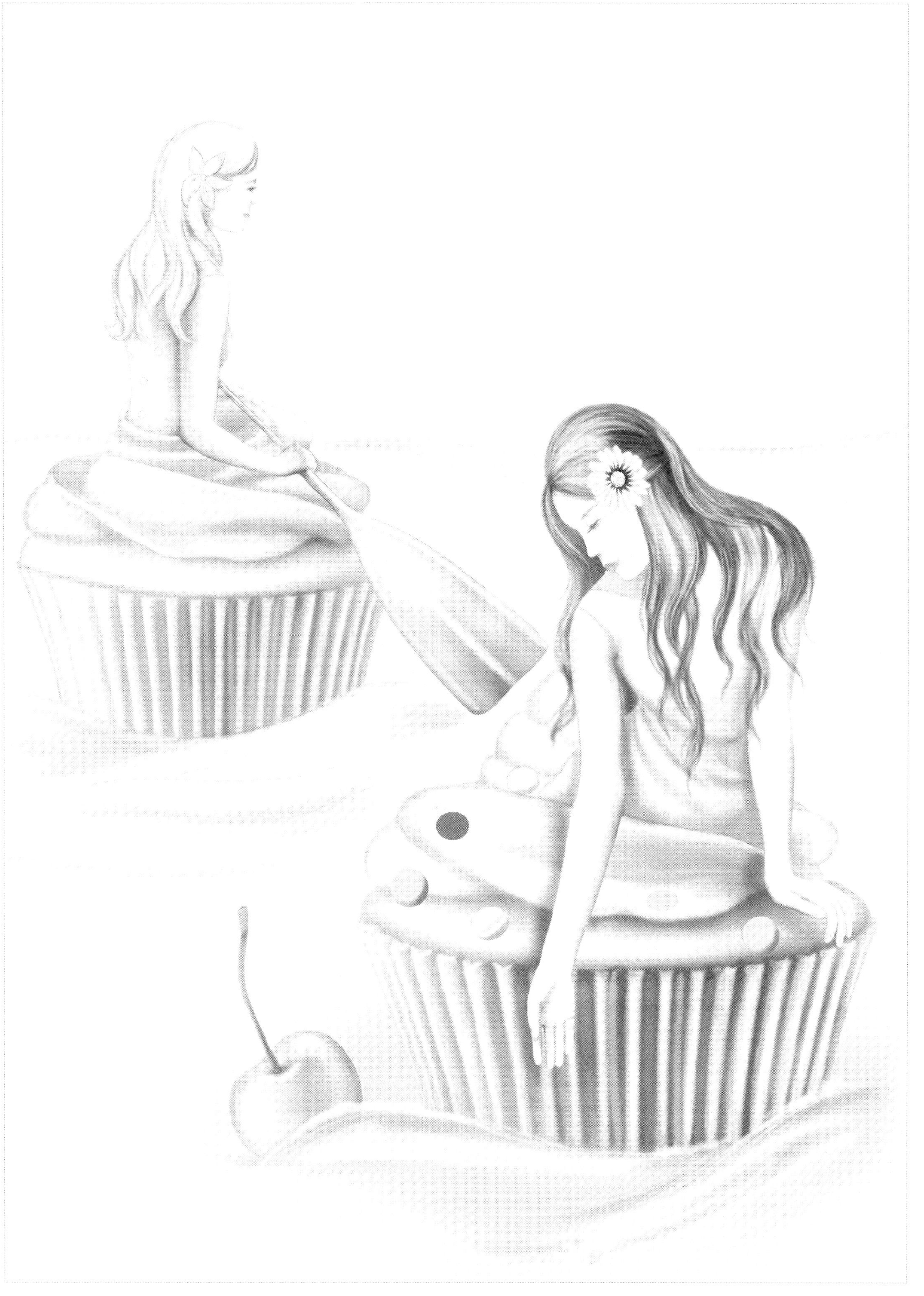

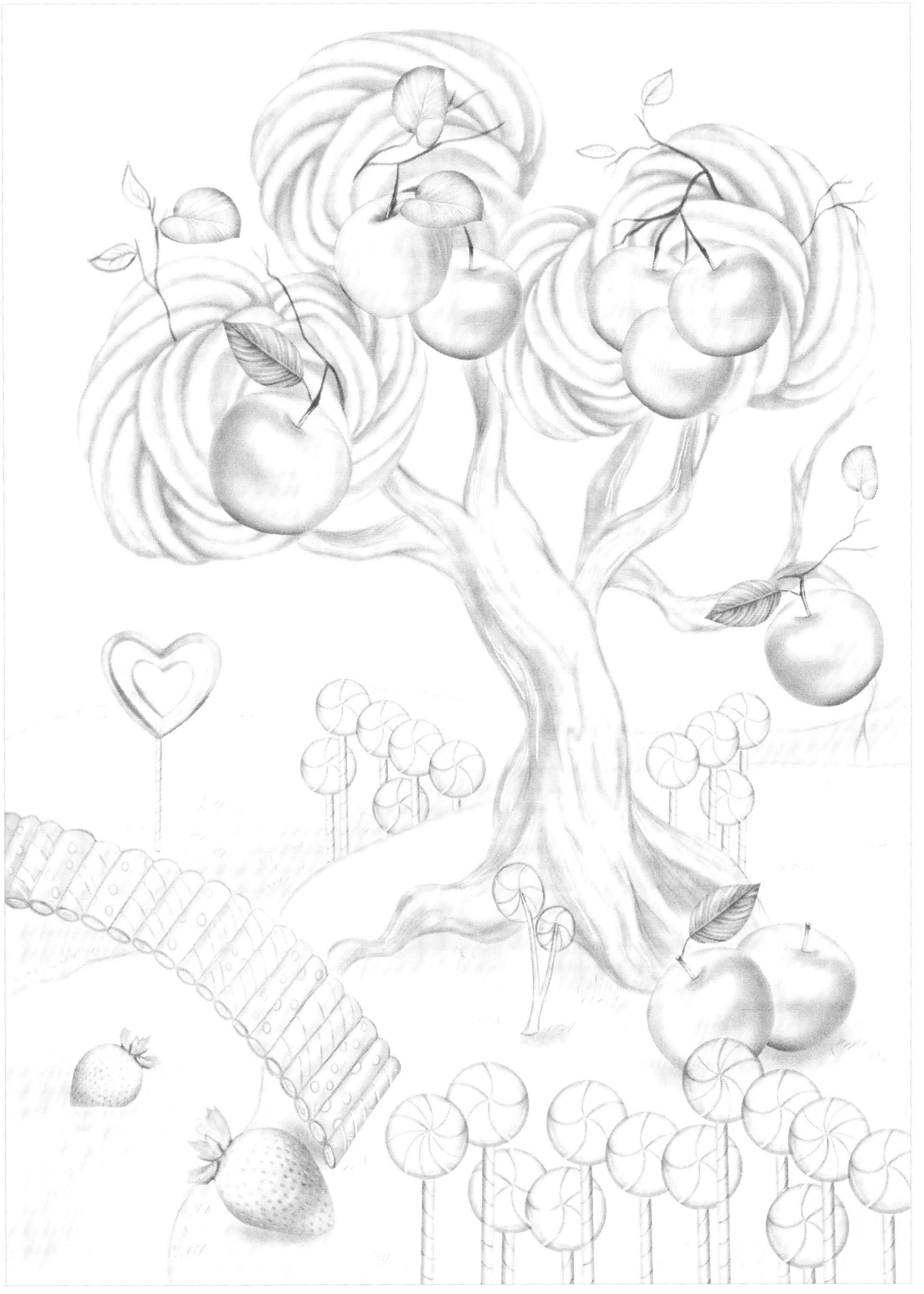

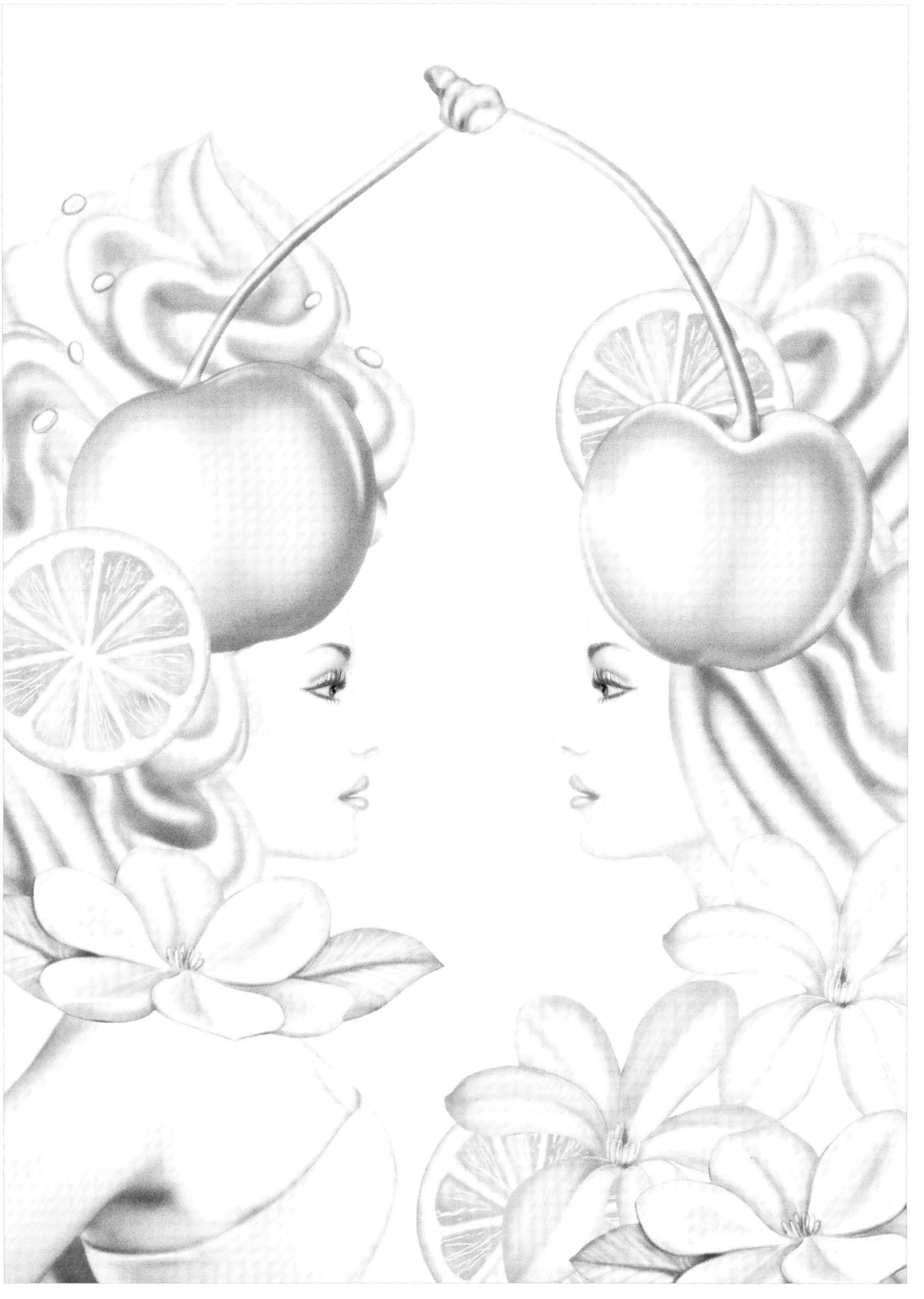

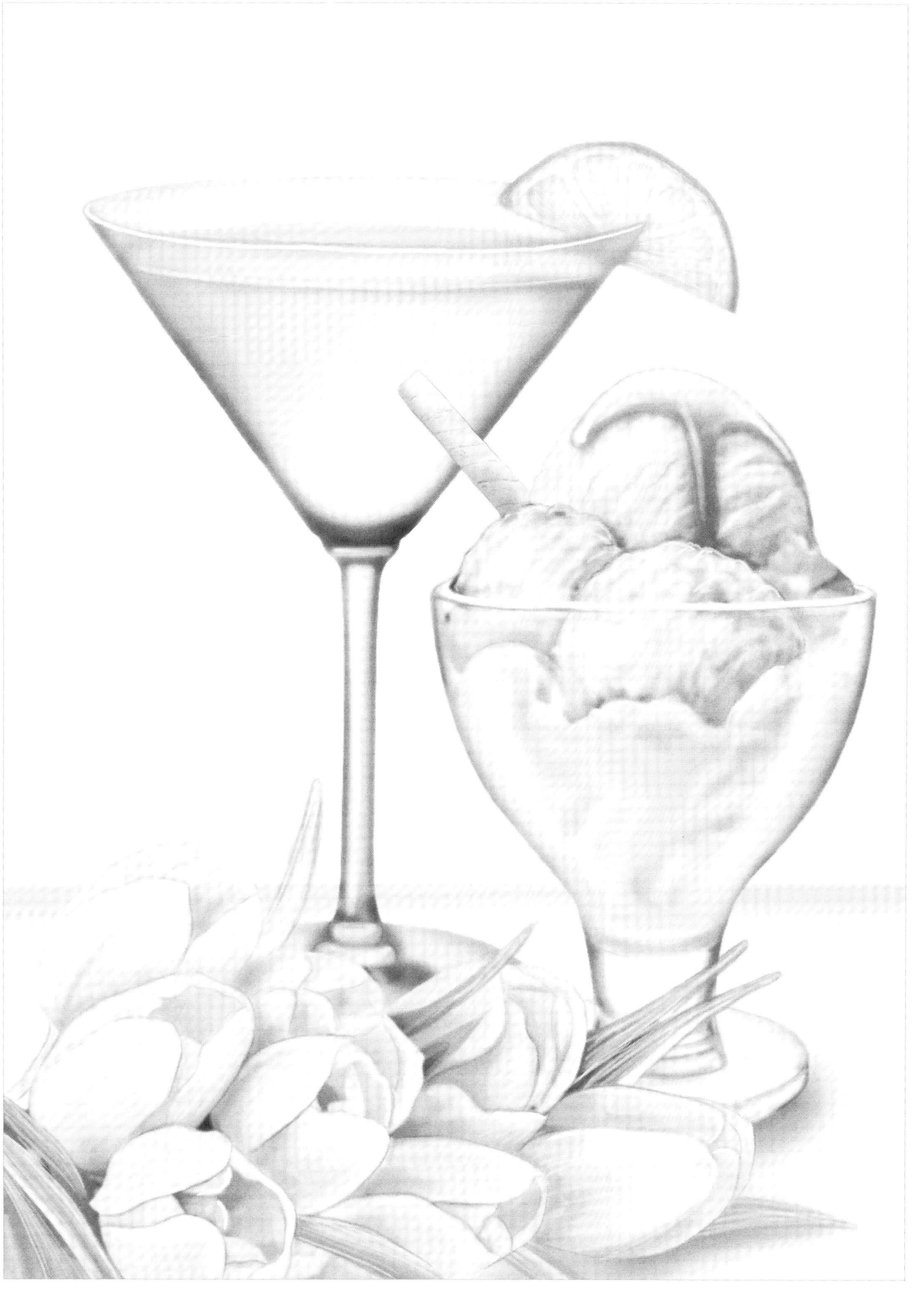

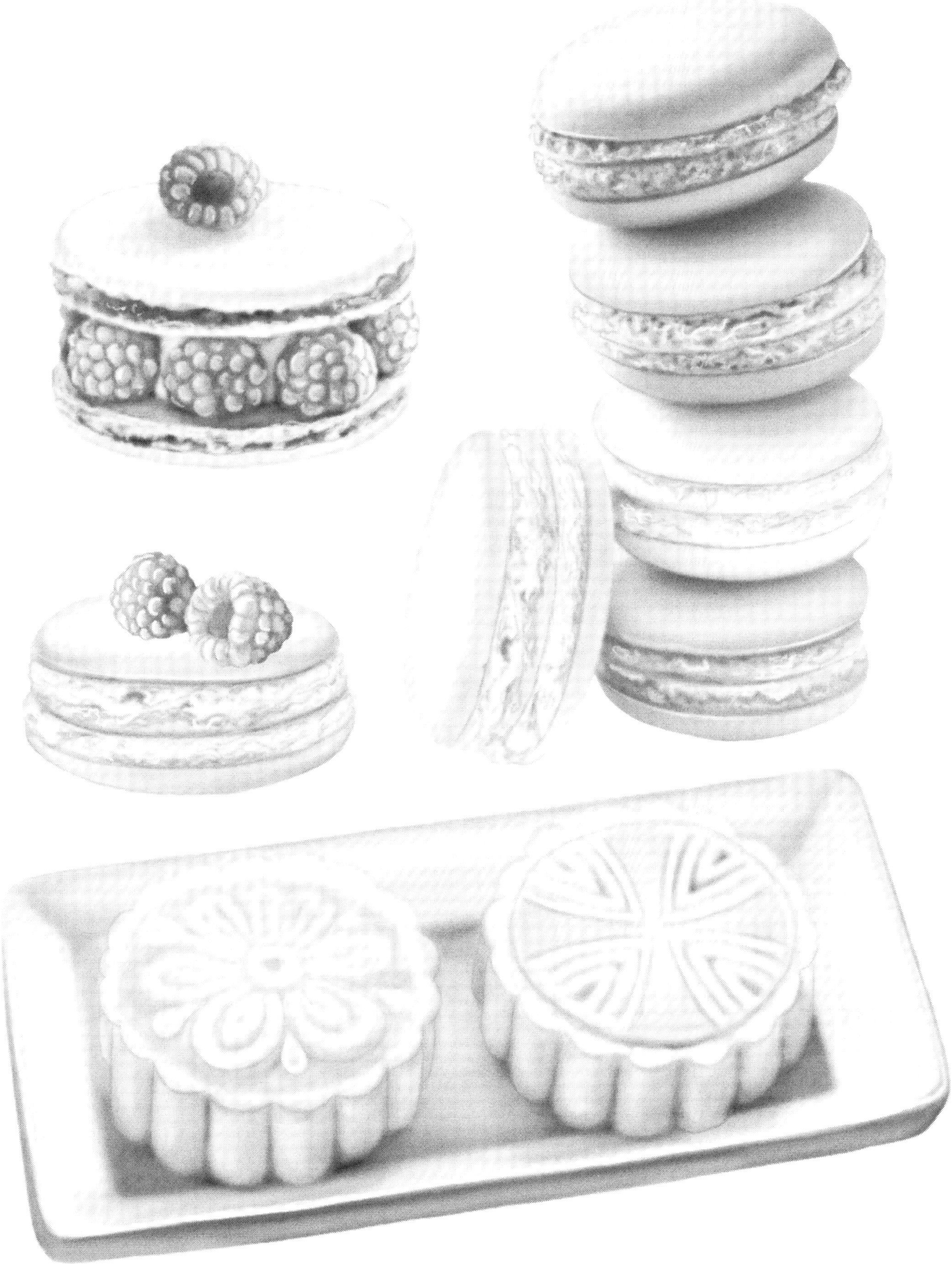

BONUS

7 of the finest greyscale pictures from my collections of seven books: Fashion, Amazing coloring book, Fantasy World, Halloween, Fashion life, Fairies, Fantasy Kingdom.

Fashion life. Coloring Book. Grayscale. By Alena Lazareva

Fashion. Coloring Book. Grayscale. By Alena Lazareva

Fantasy Kingdom. Coloring Book. Grayscale. By Alena Lazareva

Amazing Coloring Book. Grayscale. By Alena Lazareva

Fantasy World. Coloring Book. Grayscale. By Alena Lazareva

Halloween Coloring Book. Grayscale. By Alena Lazareva

Fairies. Coloring Book. Grayscale. By Alena Lazareva

Second Set of Pages begins here

Share with a family member, color with a friend
Enjoy coloring your favorite images a second time
Have an extra copy in case you make a mistake

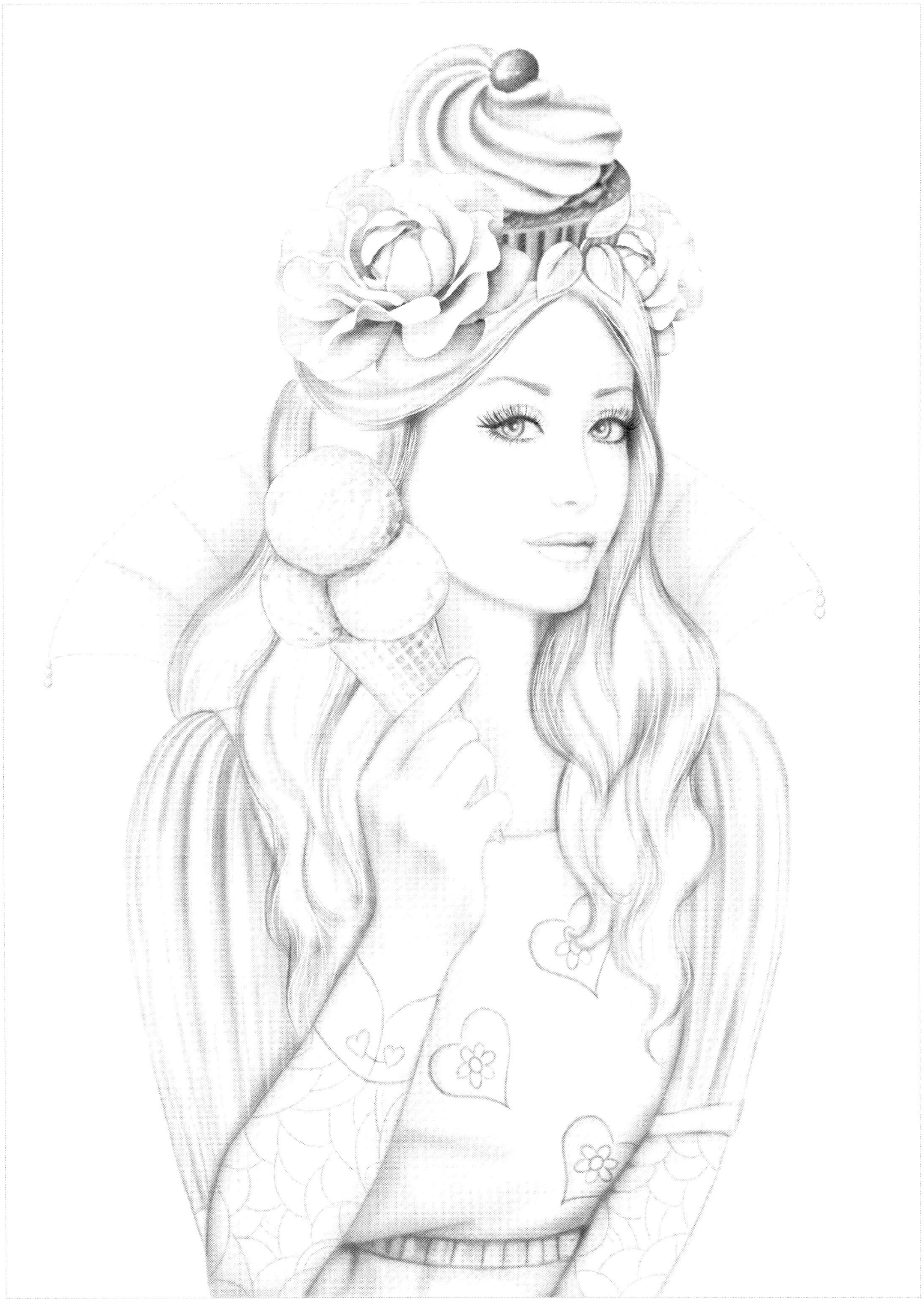

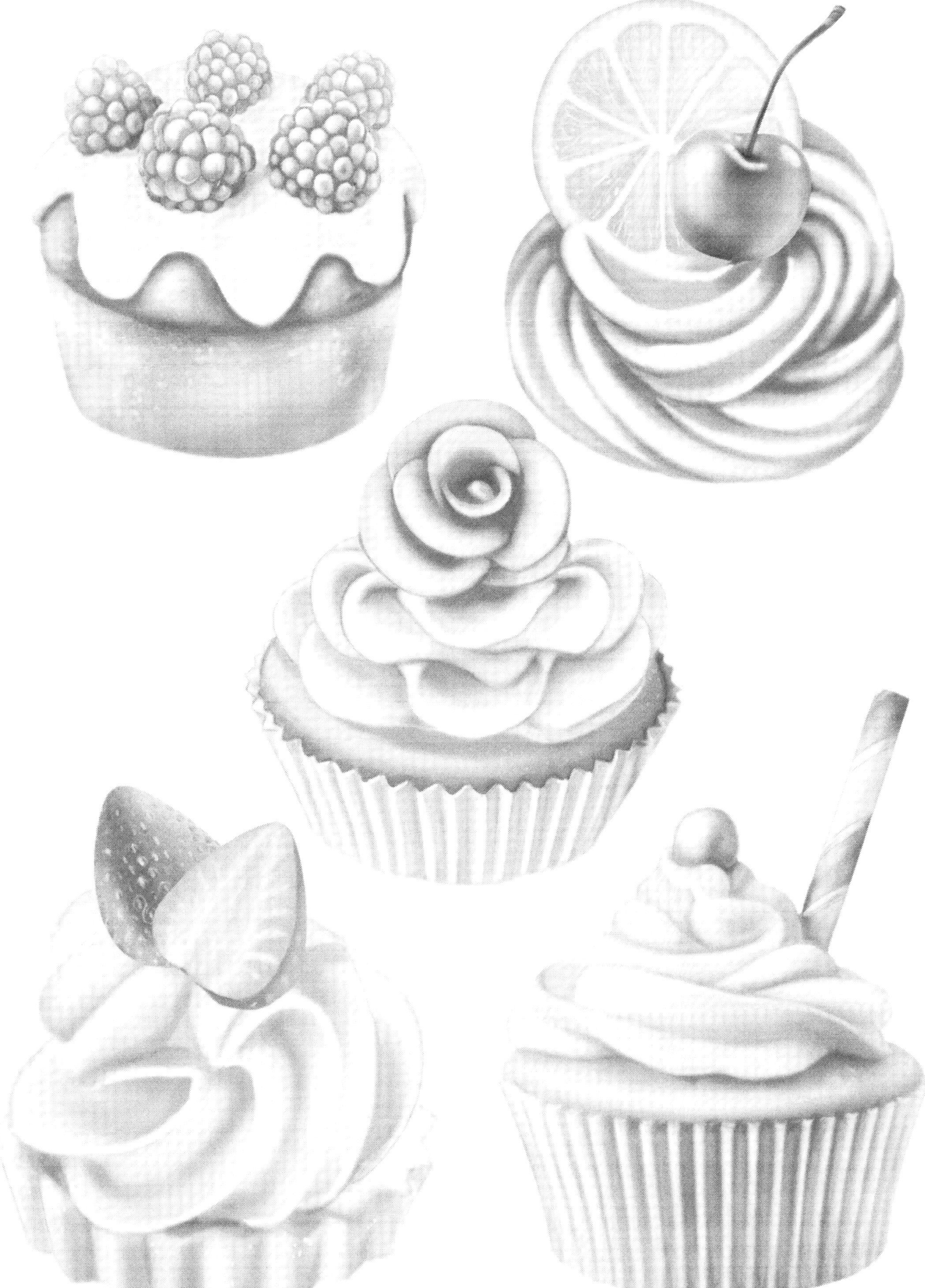

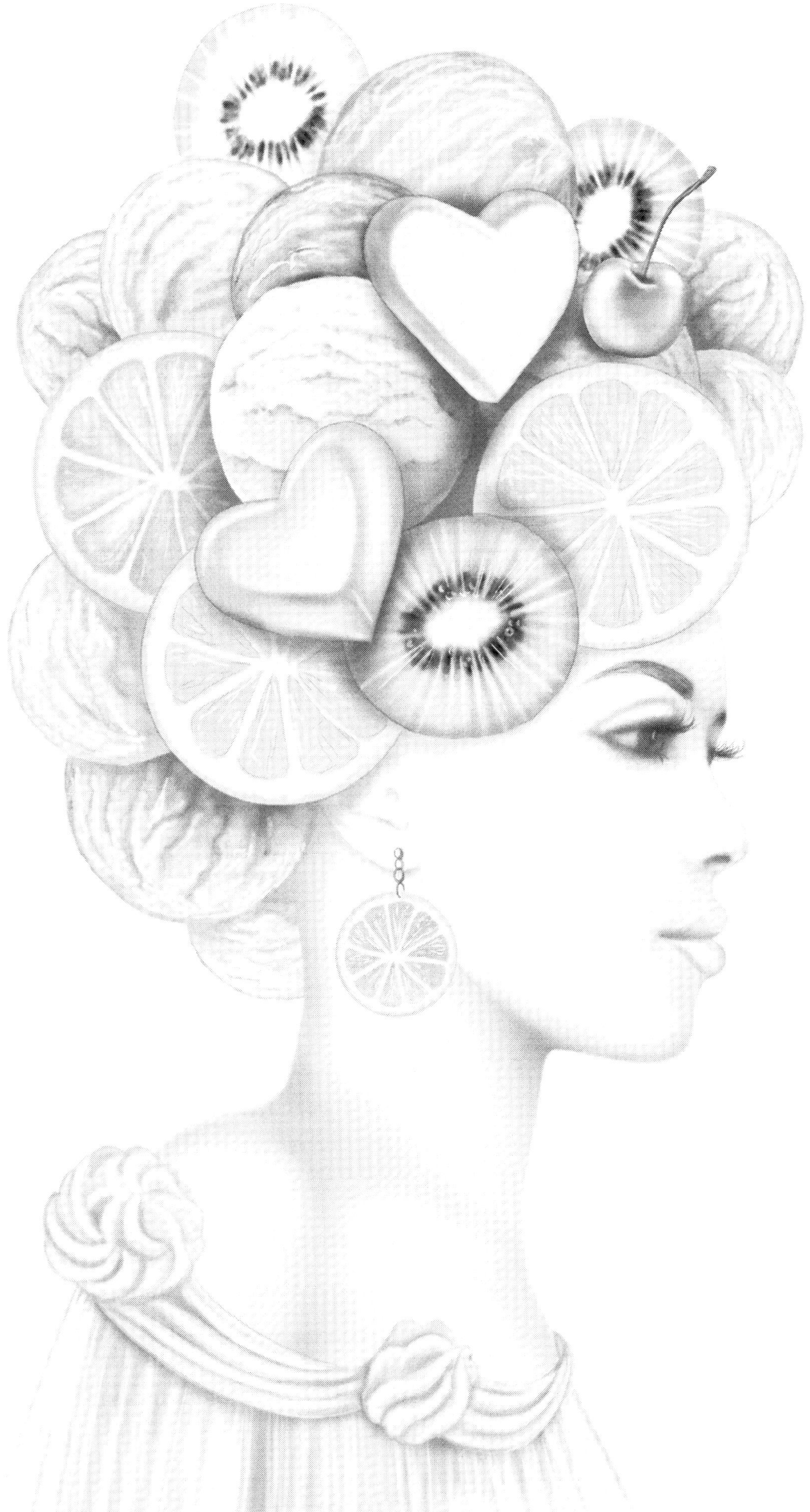

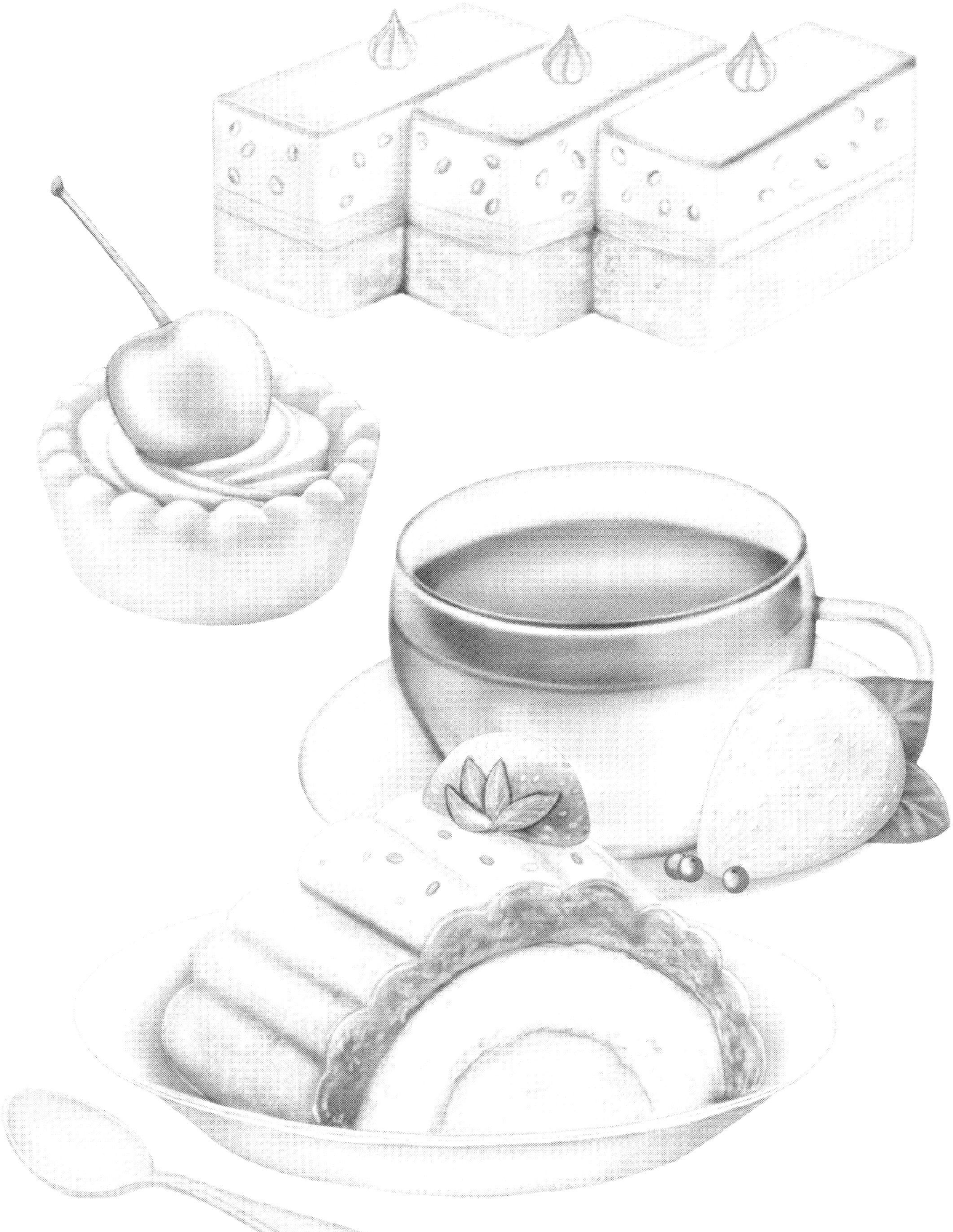

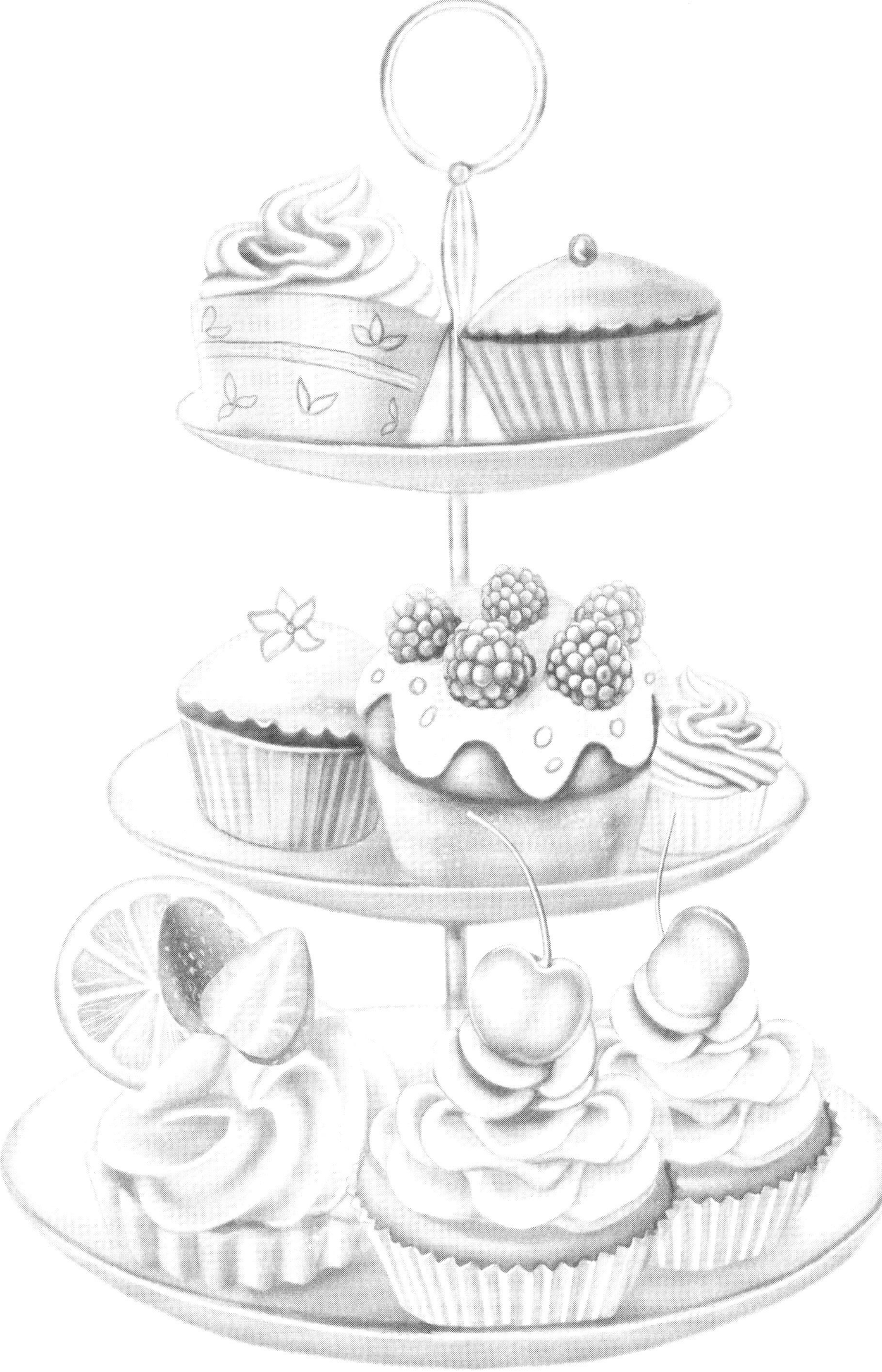

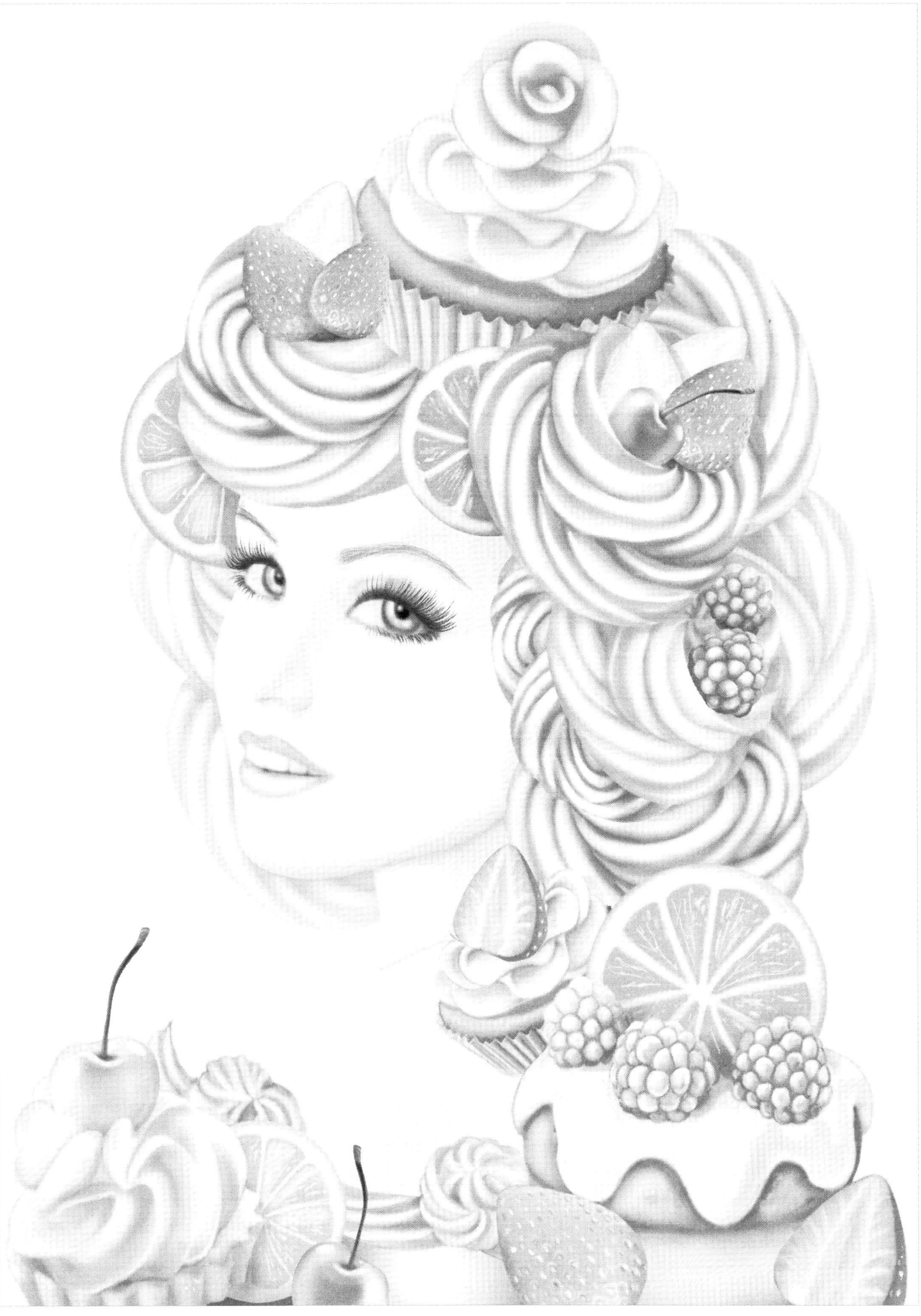

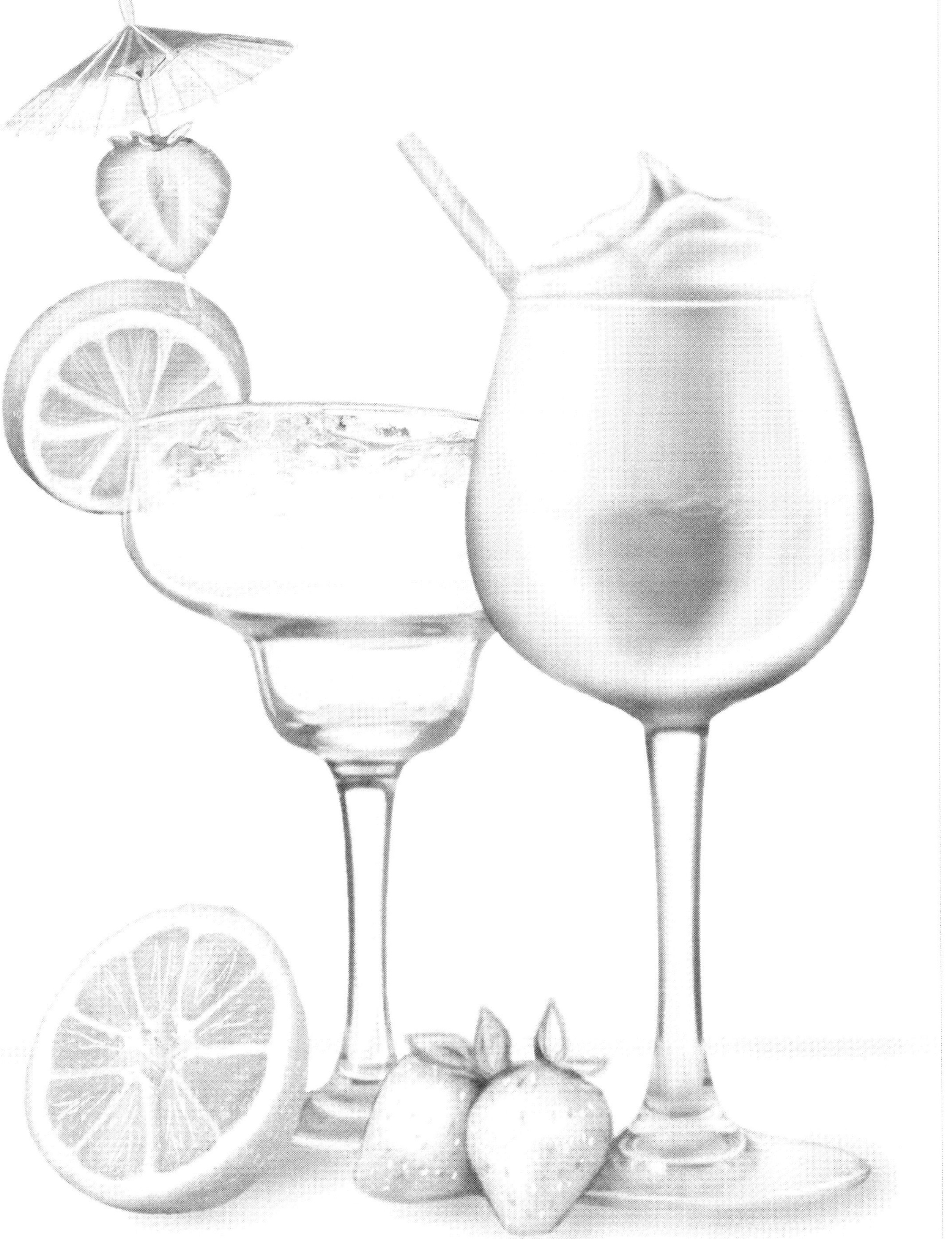

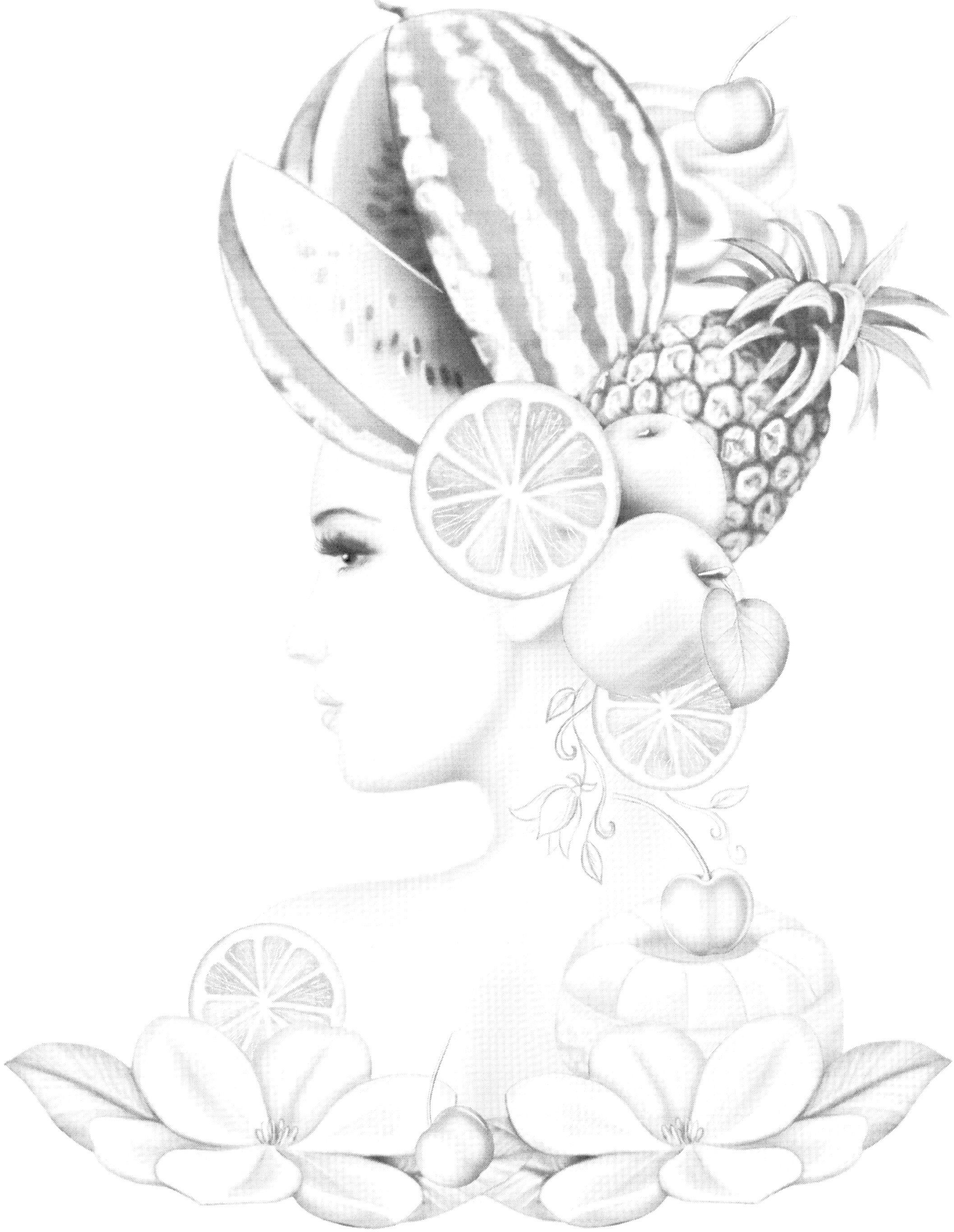

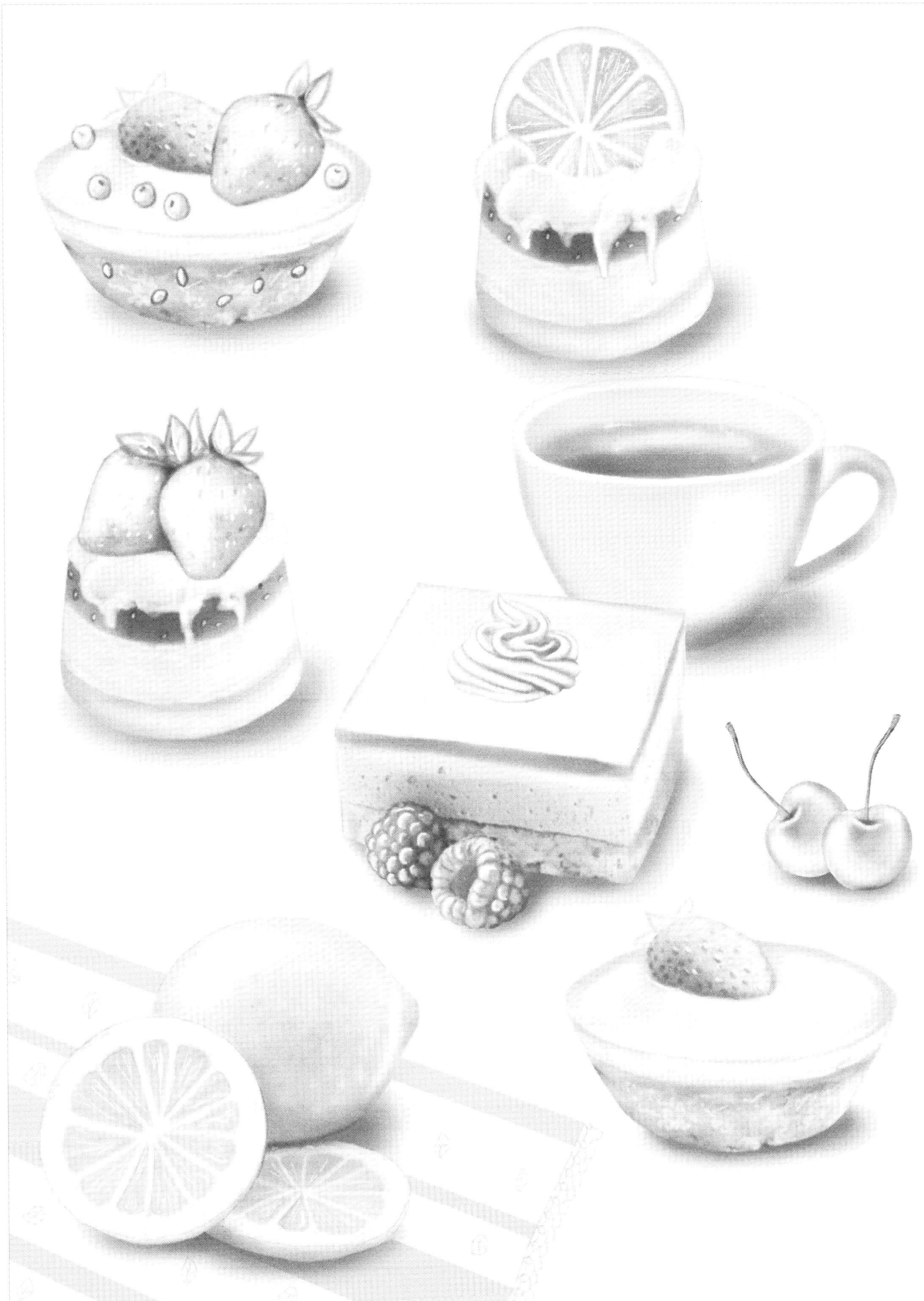

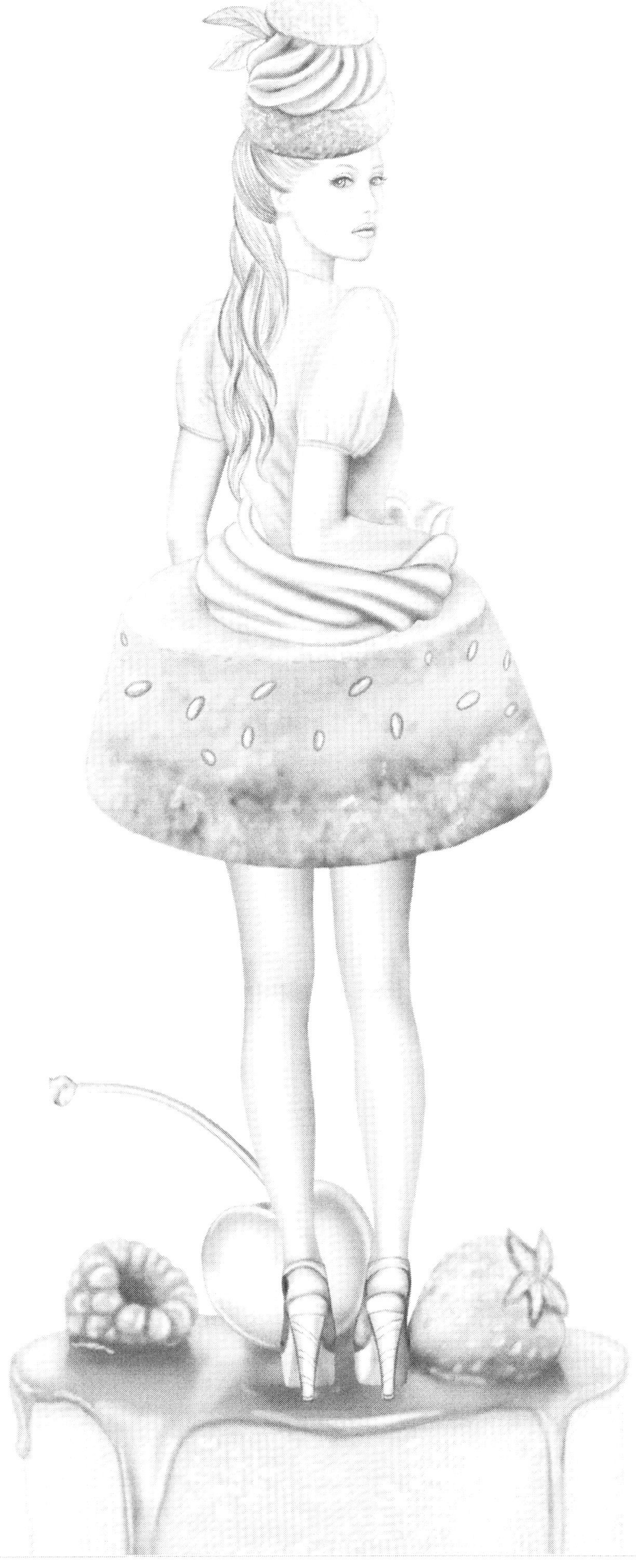

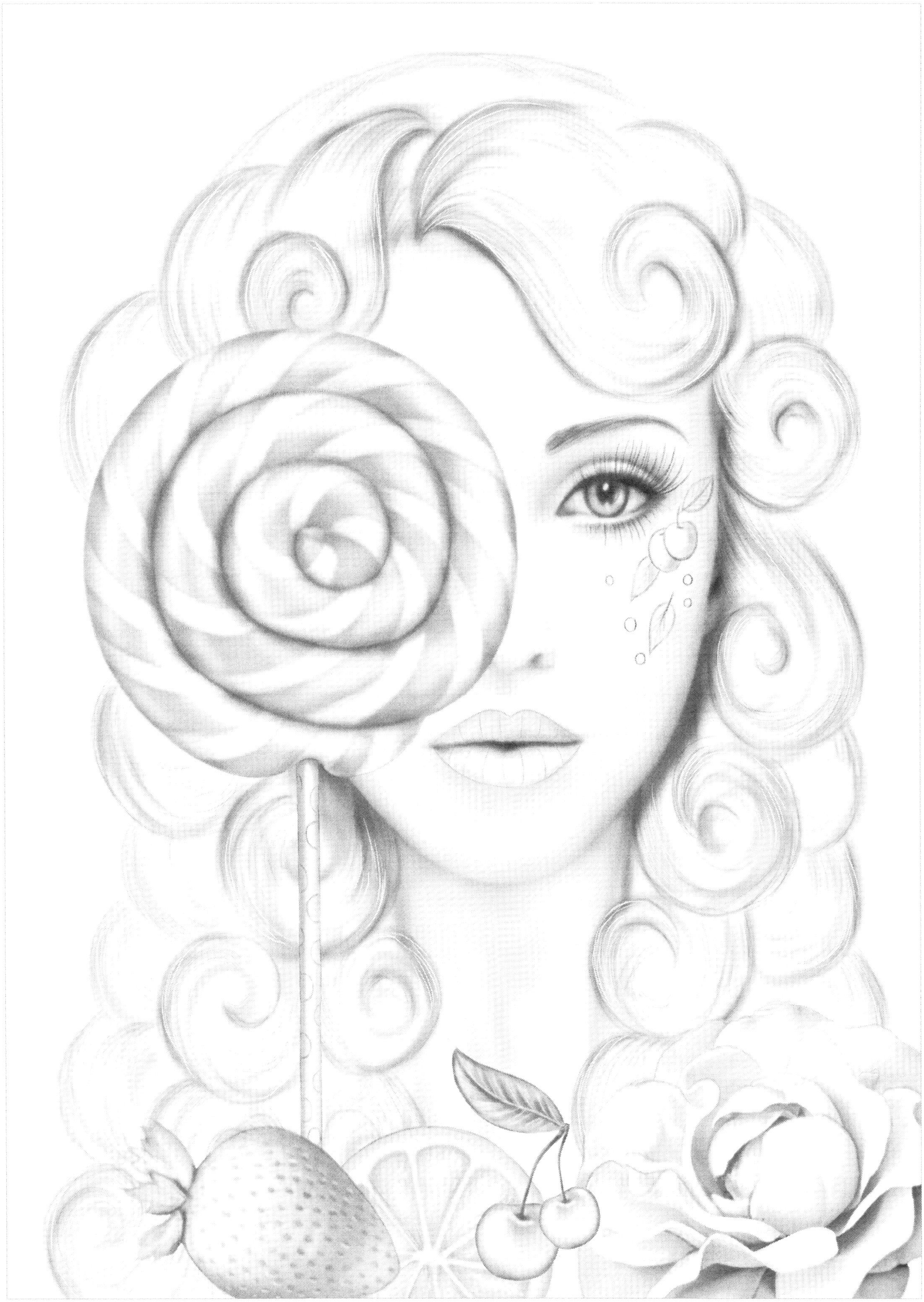

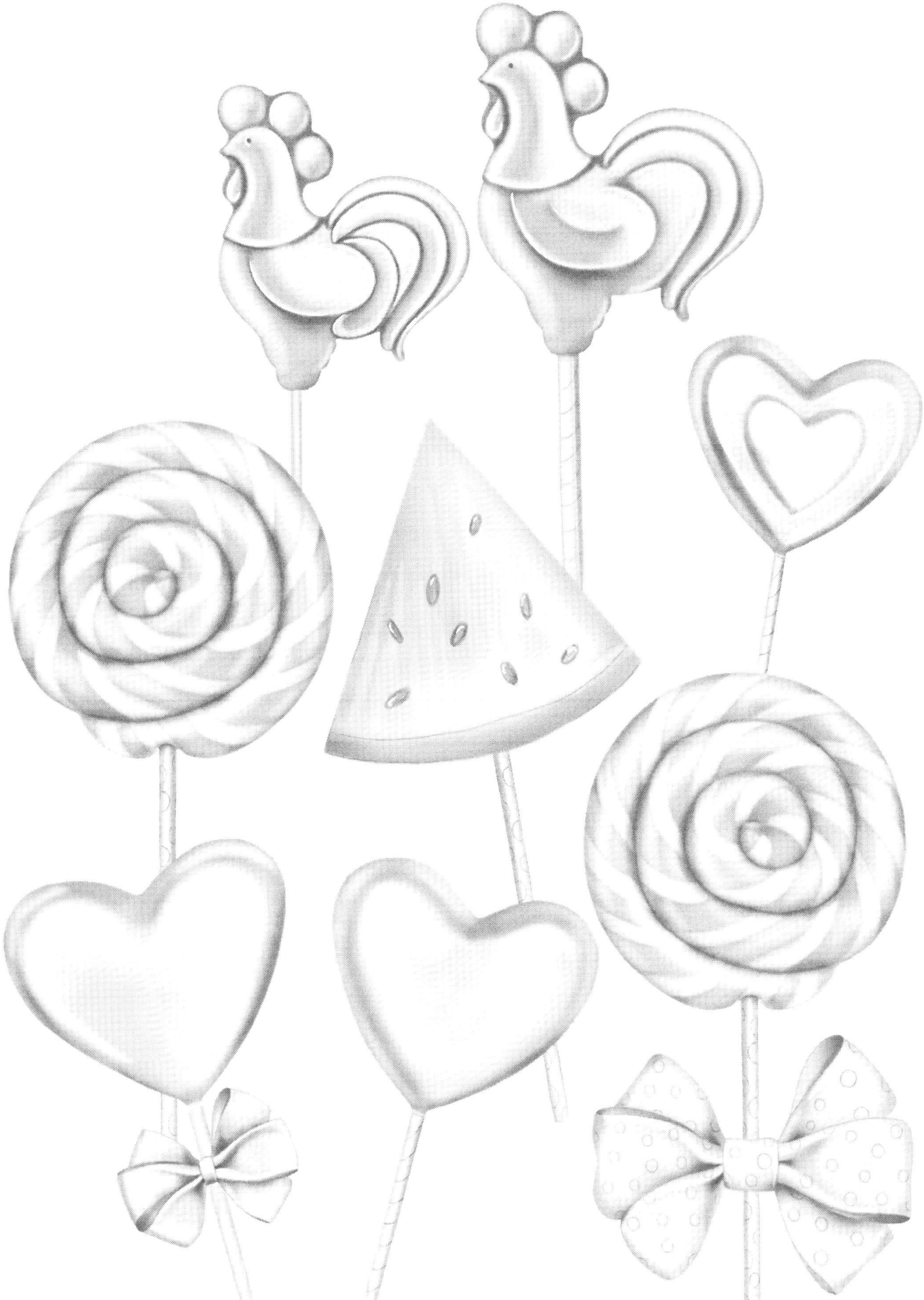

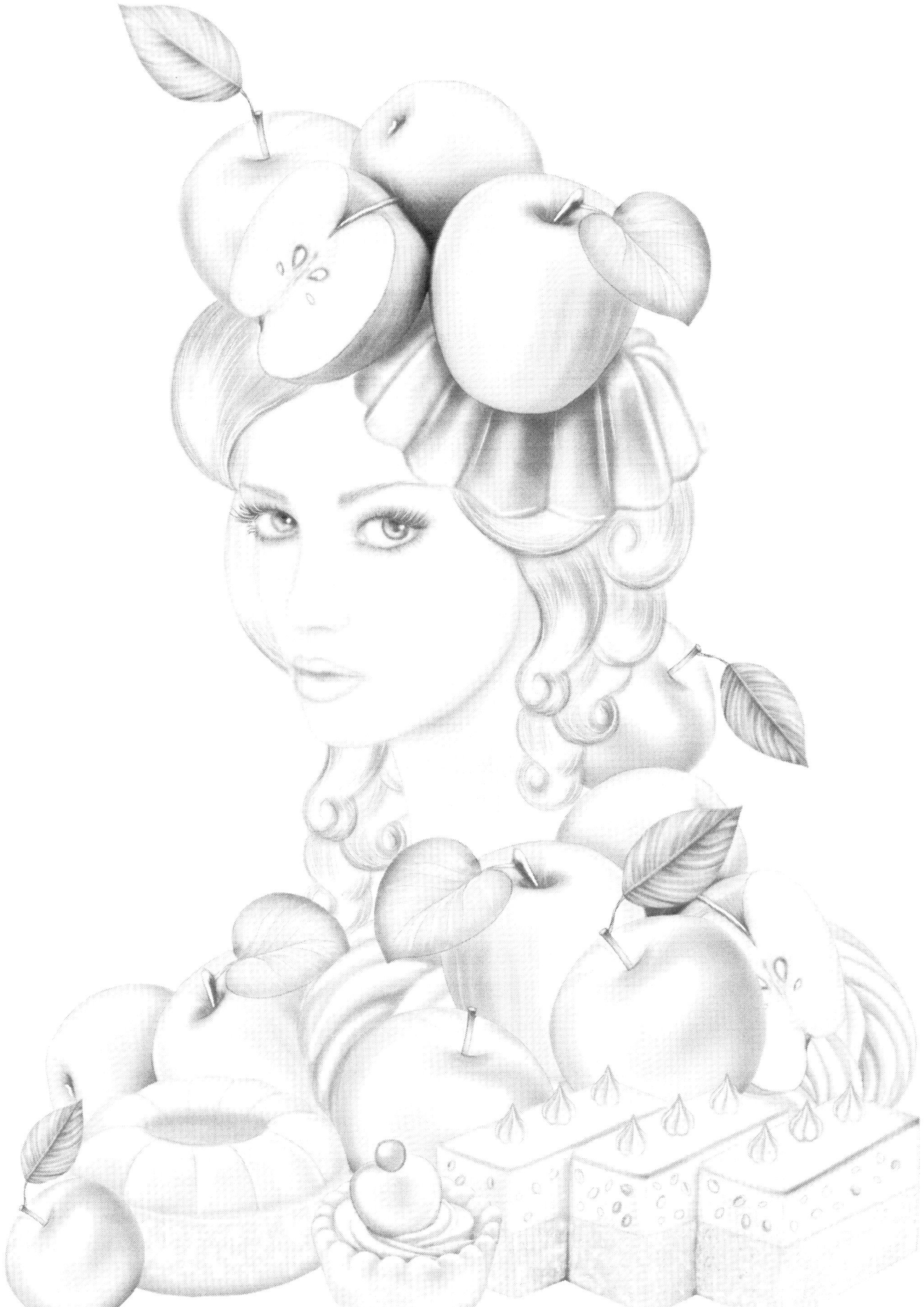

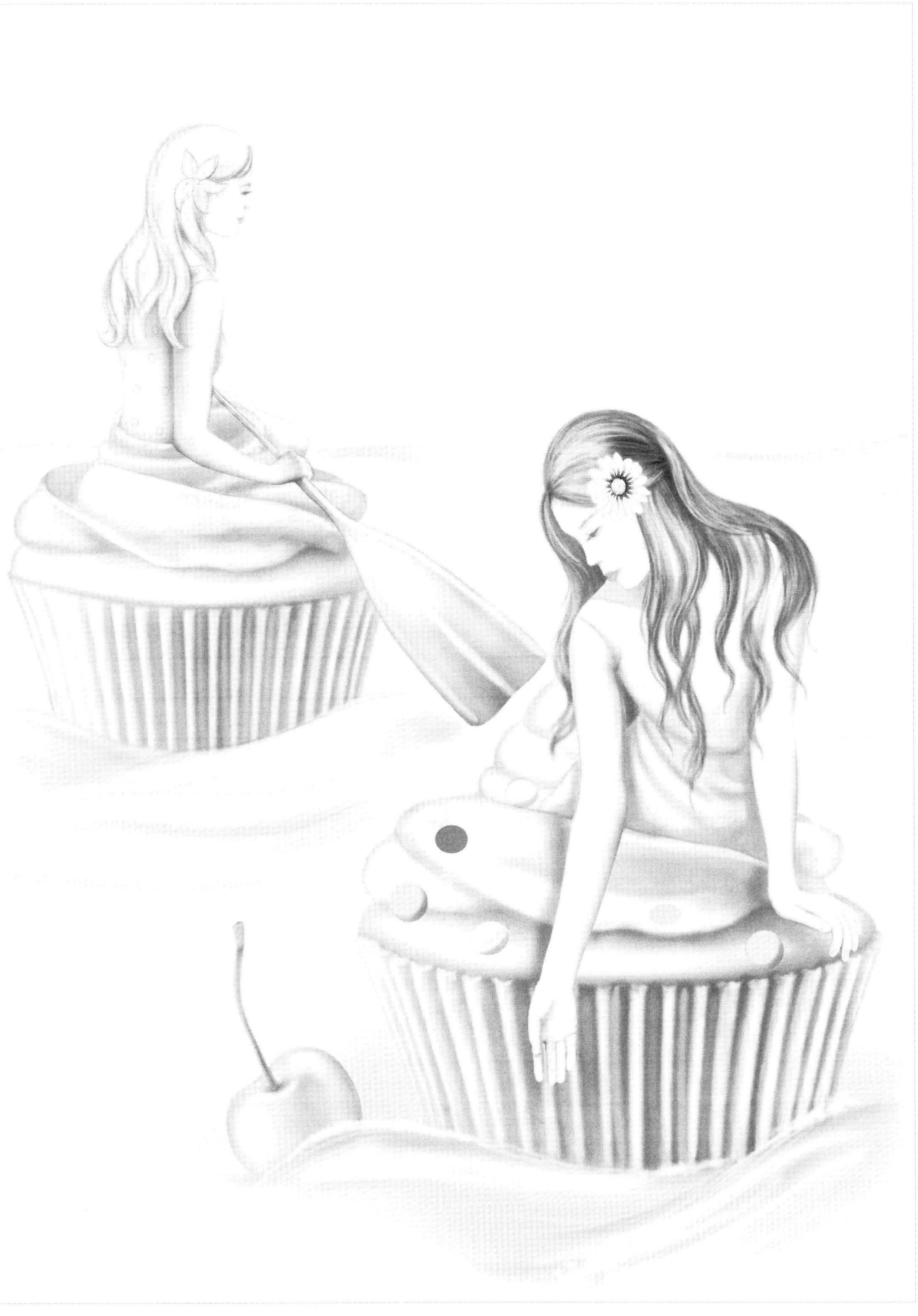

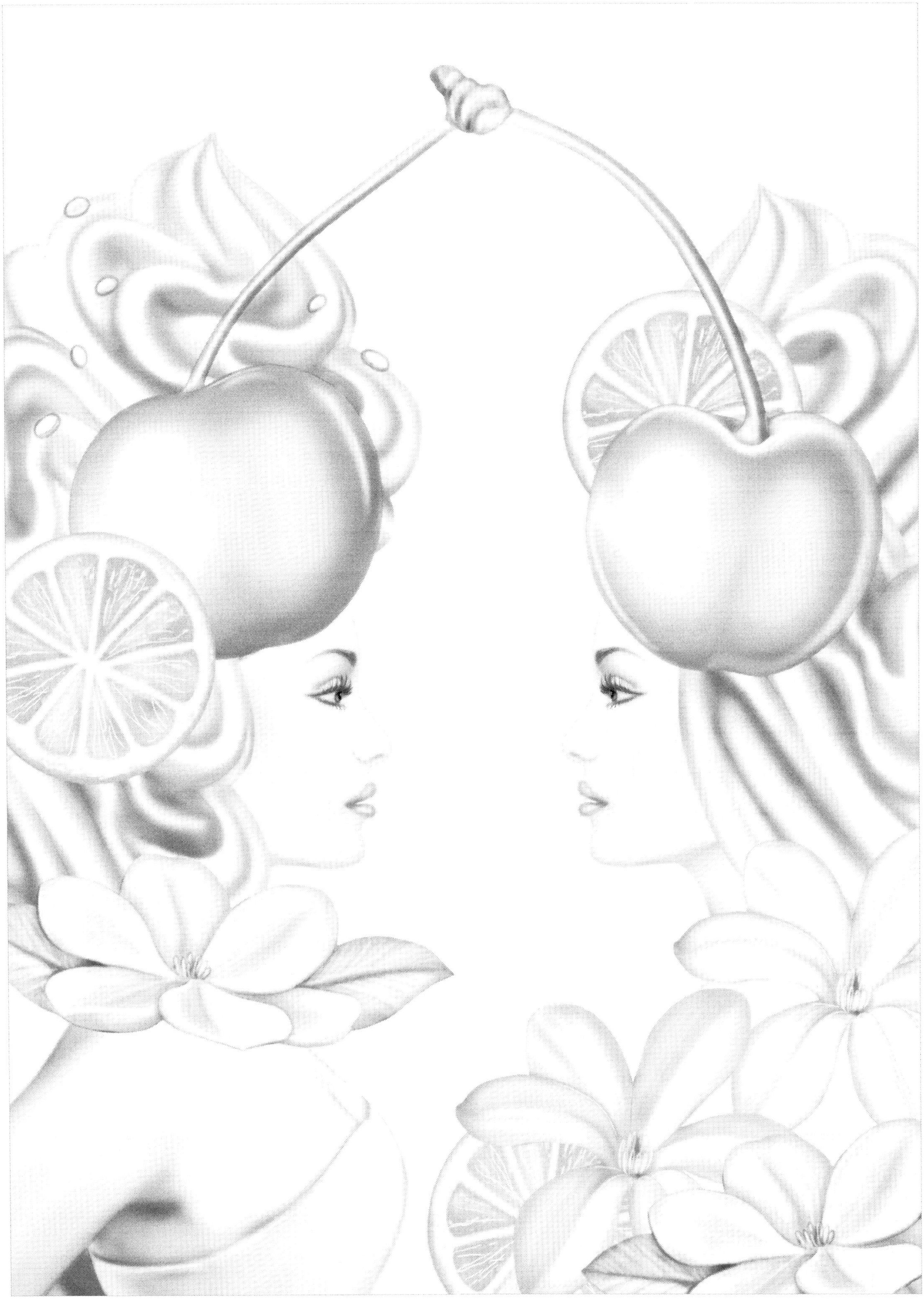

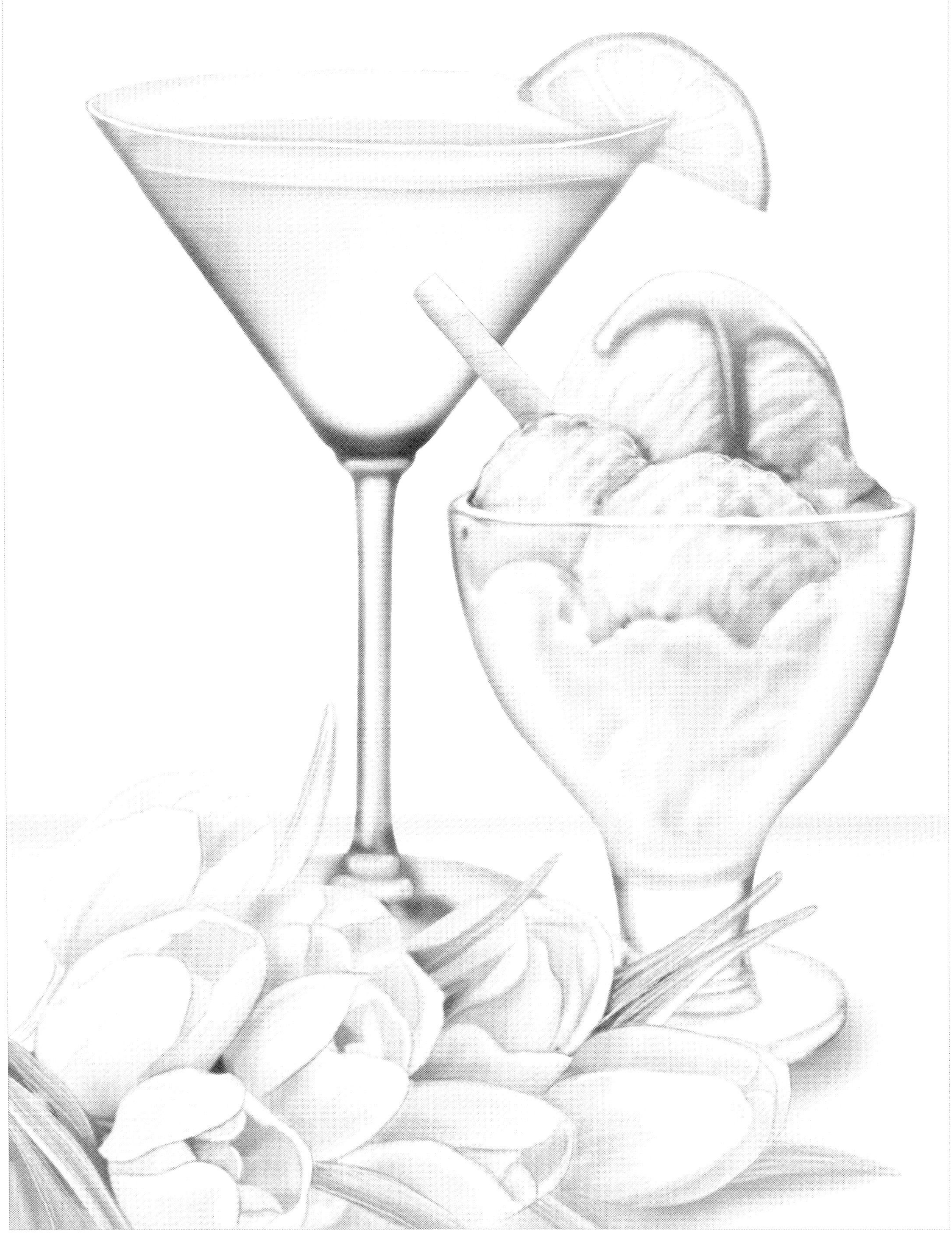

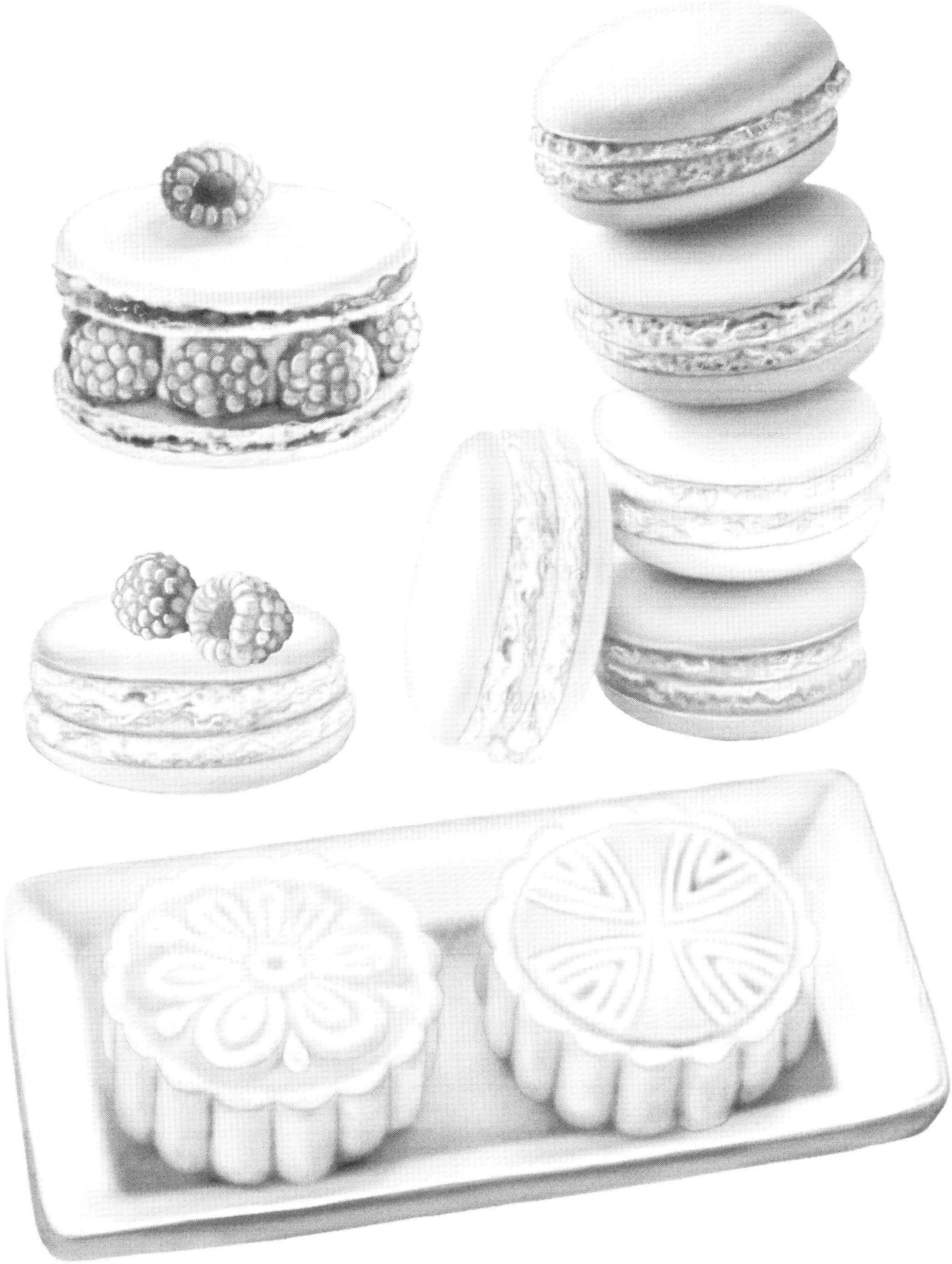

Artist

Alena Lazareva is a digital artist and illustrator. Alena Lazareva was born in Russia.

Her works had been published in magazines and books of different countries (England, Australia, Italy, Russia). Her main area of focus is fantasy art, mystical beings, fairies and mermaids.

Website: www.alenalazareva.com

Alena Lazareva also has galleries and accounts at:

facebook.com/alenalazareva.art/

instagram.com/artlazareva/

ART PRINTS

High-quality prints, posters, cards, curtains, iPhone cases, pillows, blankets, clocks, bags are available at:
www.zazzle.com/alenalazareva
www.redbubble.com/people/alenalazareva

COLORING BOOKS
by Alena Lazareva

Grayscale Coloring books

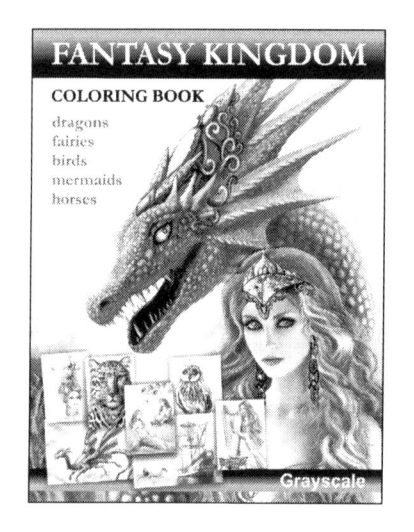

amazon

Paperback coloring books:
www.amazon.com/author/alenalazareva

Etsy

PDF (printable coloring pages and books)
www.etsy.com/shop/FantasyAlenaLazareva

Line art Coloring books

Mixed (Grayscale and Line art illustrations)

includes full color illustrations

Made in the USA
Middletown, DE
22 August 2020